D1406023

THE INCREDIBLE
LIGHTNESS
OF
BEING

Ways to Stay Lighthearted
When Life Feels Heavy

Camie J. Davis

To Kristy ~ who told me it was time
to write another book.

To Paula ~ who took my hand
and led me from the realm of
thinking into doing.

Contents

"I did not ask for success; I asked for wonder.

And you gave it to me."

Abraham Joshua Heschel

Remember to Remember

This book is not the ultimate answer nor comprehensive instructions on how to maintain lightheartedness in a world that sometimes feels heavy. Instead, it is a few tenets of faith, mindsets, and life lessons that help me be lighthearted and maintain happiness and peace and I hope that they can also help you. As my health practitioner likes to say about the remedies and supplements she recommends for her patients, this book is a piece of the puzzle of a much bigger picture. Although, I hope that what I share will be a big piece of your puzzle.

Hopefully, this book will be a springboard that propels you to take deliberate actions to be lighthearted. It will remind you that your inner life is key to what your outer life looks like and feels like, therefore, reminding you to better care for and feed your soul. And it will help you come out from under heaviness; to stop being buried under life. Some of you just need a good dusting off. Others need help being pulled out of an early grave to avoid being buried alive.

This book will, in essence, help you remember what you already know. I'm in the camp of believing the doctrine of innatism, which states that we are born with possession of certain knowledge, versus the doctrine of tabula rasa, which states that we are born as a clean slate with no built-in mental content. The Platonic doctrine of recollection says that we are born possessing all knowledge deep within and our quest in life is to "discover" that knowledge again. Judaism explains our innate knowledge with a story that says while we were in the womb an angel taught us everything we needed to know to exist in this world. Yet, just before we were born, the angel gave us a little tap between the nose and upper lip causing us to forgot everything we were taught. Thus, we began our journey in life as a quest to remember.

I believe we innately know everything we need to know. How could it be otherwise if we are connected to God? Therefore, our task is to remember. So that's what I will help you do. I will help you remember what you already know.

Many of the tenets of faith, mindsets, and life lessons I will share that help me maintain lightheartedness are rooted in the faith of Judaism. I grew up learning the teachings of Christianity, which gave me a foundation of ethics, faith, and introduced me to God as my Father. For those familiar with Christianity, you know that Jesus was quick to point out that one of his main roles was to lead people to and teach them about the Father, i.e. about God. Several years ago I was fortunate to be introduced to the teachings of Judaism, too, which expanded my knowledge and beliefs about God.

The teachings of Judaism were like walking through a door labeled, "Everything Else You Ever Wanted to Know about God." It was a doorway into learning about the infinite, vast, expansive, beyond-anything-the-mind-can-comprehend attributes of God. I love that many of the teachings in Judaism helped me get God out of the box where I had placed Him.

There are many names for and ways to refer to God. My favorite names and the ones I use in this book are God, Universe, and Source. One of the reasons I love interchanging these names is because, like I said, I've known God since I was a child. And even though I know God is God, I still understand Him and believe things about Him in limited ways. Referring to God as the Universe or Source helps my mind and heart expand to remember that He is EVERYTHING, thus, also helping me get Him out of the box.

Guess what? You just read what really should have been the preface. But since I hardly ever read a foreword or preface, I assumed you might not either, so that's why I included the preface in chapter one. Now, to the actual chapter . . .

We are incredible human beings living in an incredible

world. Sometimes, though, many of us feel anything but incredible and life feels heavy. So what can we do to remain lighthearted (have a heart radiating with light) when life feels heavy? Or is it even possible in this day-and-age to be lighthearted and to maintain happiness and peace?

Many people I know and have read things by, from spiritual mentors, family members, and friends, have expressed that life feels very heavy. They admit that they are struggling to maintain faith and optimism, much less are experiencing steadfast happiness and peace. When a friend recently described life, she said, "I'm afraid that this abnormal heaviness is becoming the new normal."

We live in a unique time in history, at least in some aspects. Unfortunately, history is rife with pain and tragedies due to wars, economic crises, corrupt governments and religious systems, plagues, poverty, famine, natural disasters, etc. What is unique now, though, is our ability to access information. Although access to copious amounts of information is an amazing, life-enhancing gift, it's also a source of constant negative information which can lead to stress and sadness. We barely have time to mourn or process a tragedy before we hear of another tragedy that has happened. The attrition from negative information adds to the stress, fears, and uncertainties we feel regarding our own problems. Sometimes the heaviness of life simply feels overwhelming.

Life doesn't have to always feel or be overwhelming, though. Life can abound with happiness and peace. I believe that we can be consistently lighthearted. But we're going to have to employ deliberate actions to feel that way. At least at first, and maybe even for a long time, we're going to have to work at being lighthearted, happy, and peaceful. Sigh. I just want lightheartedness, happiness, and peace - all the feel goods - to be automatic by-products of existing. And maybe they can be. Maybe lightheartedness, happiness, and peace can be as automatic as breathing. But first, for most of us, it's going to take some work, okay a lot of work, to get to that point.

Working at maintaining lightheartedness is akin to being a good athlete. Consider a basketball player who has an amazing, accurate shot, who can score from anywhere on the court even when he's being tightly defended. When a great player shoots and scores it often looks automatic. And when he's making a high percentage of his shots it seems magical. It's called being "in the zone." But hundreds, even thousands of hours of practice precede a shot becoming accurate and automatic.

We need to be like athletes who are dedicated to practicing. Especially those of us who have developed patterns of negative reactions to the events in life. I believe we can get "in the zone" of being lighthearted and stay there most of the time. But it will require dedicated work to remember how to replace negative patterns with positive emotions, positive actions, and faith.

Lastly, although I want to help you be lighthearted, my motive is not solely to help you. Universal redemption comes through personal, individual experiences and evolutions. What you do matters. Your life has a ripple effect and you never know how far-reaching those ripples will be. If I can somehow help you, it will help others, which will help the world. So let's do something together. Let's create lightheartedness in our own lives which in turn will affect everyone around us and literally make the world a lighter place.

Remember to Love Yourself

First things first. The things I share in this book will not help you, long-term, if you don't first and foremost love yourself. Wait! Don't stop reading. I'm not talking about a sugar-coated or self-absorbed kind of love. I'm talking about a raw, strong, necessary kind of love that wells up from the depths of your being. Because if you don't love yourself, it is impossible to love others in a healthy way. And loving yourself and others in a healthy way is a key to being lighthearted (having a heart radiating with light).

Do you love yourself? Here's one litmus test that will indicate whether you love yourself in a healthy way and, therefore, love others in a healthy way. Here's the big question: Are you perpetually judgmental? If you answered yes, then I'm afraid that you don't really love yourself. Because the root of perpetually judging others stems from judging yourself. And people who love themselves don't judge themselves. At least, not in an unhealthy way. True story. An aversion toward others is often an outward manifestation of how we feel about ourselves.

People who love themselves do have an inner critic that can lead to criticism and judgment of themselves and of others. But it's constructive criticism and judgment, based on love rather than disdain, that leads to self-improvement rather than leading to guilt, feelings of unworthiness, or even worse self-hatred. Unhealthy judgments are based on a condemning, critical attitude rather than on a genuine concern for the well-being of others, and stems from disdain for oneself that spills over into condemning and judging others. Whew, that was a long sentence, but an even longer life sentence if you're someone who lives that way.

So let's open our hearts in the deepest way and remember to love ourselves. This chapter will most likely be a springboard for you. It will prompt you to start thinking about loving yourself if you don't already do so. Once you have a desire and an intention to love yourself, you'll find that the Universe will lead you to just the right people, books, scriptures, teachings, experiences, etc., that will help you establish and maintain a healthy love for yourself. The Universe is so nice in that way; always for us and in our favor.

To help you start loving yourself, I'm going to remind you of how beautiful you are. So here goes: You are so beautiful. No, really. You are absolutely beautiful. Not only are you beautiful, but you're amazing too. If you really believe that, it will change everything. Everything.

Yet, I also need to remind you that you are nothing.

Absolutely nothing. And if you really believe that, it will change everything. Everything.

So, you are beautiful and amazing but are absolutely nothing, too. How can you be both? You are both because you are an aspect of God, an extension of Him. That makes you so beautiful and amazing, yet nothing on your own.

You.

Are.

A.

Part.

Of.

God.

Stop and let that sink in. The purpose of creation is to provide a dwelling place for God. You do that. That makes you beautiful and amazing. You are a dwelling place for God. A conduit. A vessel. His unique expression. His unique way of interacting with the world that He can only do through you. I hope you can somewhat grasp how incredibly fantastic and awe-inspiring that makes you.

Yet, that's also what makes you nothing. You are nothing apart from God. No part of you exists outside of Him. We live, move, and have our being in Him. One of the deepest teachings of Judaism and in some other faiths is that the only reality is God. He is *Ein Sof,* the Endless One. There is nothing else outside of Him. So you are literally nothing outside of Him.

Long ago, Rabbi Simcha Bunim of Poland always carried two slips of paper with him, one in each pocket. On one slip of paper was written, "For my sake, the world was created." On the other was written, "I am but dust and ashes." It was a way for him to be balanced by remembering that he was everything, yet nothing.

One of my favorite memories is when my three year-old son walked up to me while I was putting on my makeup and asked, "Momma, if God stopped existing would we stop existing too?" (Yes, he really talked that way when he was that young.) I chuckled and hugged him while my heart exploded a little bit because he was catching a glimpse of how big God was, and answered, "Yes, we would just stop existing."

Everything we do, down to each breath we take, is a gift and an intervention from God. We are nothing without Him. We are everything because of Him. And that is the core, fundamental reason that we should love ourselves - because we are extensions of God in unique, one-of-a-kind ways.

Even though I don't use the greeting, I love how some people greet each other by bowing slightly and saying "Namaste." By saying that, they are acknowledging the Light/God in each other, and if for no other reason, that would be reason enough to honor and recognize the worth of an individual. Saying "Namaste" is a beautiful example of seeing God in others and treating them accordingly, as if that is all we see. Because if you don't remember, let me remind you of the way God looks at us. He sees all of our good and focuses on that instead of focusing on our "bad." He's the One True Judge. So if He chooses to focus on our good, who are we to focus on the "bad" in people? There is nothing more powerful than a person who knows his or her worth. And the root of our worth, that can't be easily taken away from us once that it's grasped, is that we are extensions of our Creator.

It's time for me to be vulnerable. Deep breath. I just recently started loving myself. Yep, it's true. Don't misunderstand. I didn't hate myself, or even dislike myself. But I didn't actually love myself, at least not unconditionally. Which is kind of surprising because I'm basically a well-rounded, healthy person whose had a good life. But I judged myself more than I loved myself. Bottom line, I had to qualify for my own love.

Do you know what my I-have-to-qualify-for-my-own-love ran parallel with? With how I felt about God. Yes, I was taught that God's love is unconditional. I knew that, but I didn't really *know* it. I didn't believe it for myself. I had to do the right things to earn His love.

11

Experiencing unconditional love from God and for myself entered my life via a Reiki session. If you are unfamiliar with Reiki, you might want to do a little research about it. My job and/or desire is not to convince those of you with a Western mindset of Reiki's validity. What I will say is that Reiki has led to amazing, positive changes and healing for myself, family members, and many of my close friends. It has been a source of healing and unexpectedly, a source of self-love.

During one of my Reiki sessions, the practitioner talked to me about unconditional love. She recognized that I did not accept it from God and did not feel it for myself. One of the steps she encouraged me to implement to help me get to the point of accepting unconditional love from God and for myself is as follows:

She asked if I had anyone in my life who I felt loved me unconditionally. Someone who no matter what I did, I mean *no matter what*, would still love me. A few people immediately came to mind, but one barely edged out the others, so I chose her. Each time I prayed, I was to imagine her greeting me with the love she had for me and to imagine how she demonstrated her love toward me. Whenever I visualized her greeting me and being so happy to see me, I was then supposed to visualize God greeting me that same way.

Do you remember seeing the iconic picture of Princess Diana on a yacht greeting her two sons after being away from them? She practically flew to her sons with a huge smile on her face and with her arms wide open and engulfed them in a hug. The love and enthusiasm captured in the image are palpable. This is the type of moment the Reiki practitioner wanted me to experience with God. She wanted me to feel His intense love and enthusiasm toward me each time I approached Him.

It was an amazing gift that the visualizations led to just that. Within a short period I wasn't greeted by the image of my dear friend anymore when I prayed. Instead, I felt God greet me with unconditional love each time I prayed. Hugging is my love language. So feeling God greet me with a big bear-hug was a pivotal moment for me.

Guess what happened soon after the God bear-hug moment? Guess who showed up to greet me with unconditional love, too? I did. And I have to admit, that felt extremely good.

Warning: once you open your heart with the intention to receive unconditional love, even if it's a microscopic opening, unconditional love is going to find a way to get in. So get ready. I promise it will happen. And God and your true self can't wait for that moment.

There were important concurrent events happening in my

life that helped me reach this point, but the on-going visualization was one of the biggest steps to help me love myself. As this process happened, I wrote about a conversation I had with someone encouraging her to love herself. I called the conversation, *Total Recall of Your Beautiful Self*. It went as follows:

The best kind of friends are those with whom you can be painstakingly honest. Those you can tell exactly what they need to hear, for their own good, even if it's hard for them to hear it. I had to have a painstakingly honest, heart-to-heart kind of talk recently with a friend. I'm going to let you in on our one-sided conversation because maybe you need to hear what I said. Here's the jest of what I told her:

"When did you start being so inconsequential in your own life? When did everyone else start being more important than you?

"When did you apologize for the first time? Not for a mere action that merited an apology. No, I'm wondering when you began apologizing for the person you are. When and why did you let the scales tip? When did you begin measuring yourself according to your so-called failures and mistakes versus all the other good things you do day-in-and-day-out?

"You know where these questions are leading don't you? I'm

basically asking, *when did you stop loving yourself?*

She looked away, sighed, but did not answer, so I took the liberty to continue.

"You've become inarticulate to your own narrative. You've become illiterate to your own story. So I'm going to remind you what your story is. Feel free to stop me if you think I'm getting the story wrong.

"But as I remind you of your story, you're going to remember something. You're going to remember who you are. We'll call it 'total recall.' You're going to remember how strong you are and how good it feels to be undiminished. And you're going to make an armistice with yourself suspending all hostilities toward yourself.

"I know you get tired. But how could you not get tired? You are a J.D. Salinger woman. You know the one. The one 'who holds the entire universe together.' That's a big job. But you do it well.

"You are a Steinbeck woman, too. The one 'who a kind of light spreads from causing everything to change colors. Who allows others to awaken to good days. Who makes the world better for a little tribe of people who depend on you even when they don't acknowledge their dependence.'

"You are an alchemist causing everything that you touch to glitter and be golden. You stir magic into the mundane and wonder into the ordinary. You know how to mix all of life's strange and wonderful ingredients together so well.

"You are light. Pure, unadulterated light. No, really, that is your essence. The sun is jealous of your radiance. You are that powerful, when you let yourself be.

"It's time to pull the drawstring, lifting the curtains from the windows of your soul. People miss seeing the light. But most of all, you miss shining. You are full of exceptionally large amounts of energy and light. It's time again to be the radiant being that you are.

"Most of all, you are beautiful. Oh, I know, you feel like a shape-shifter when you look at yourself in the mirror. Time and gravity have a way of changing things. But I wish that you could focus on the heart beating behind the 'non-perfect' breasts. That heart doesn't just keep blood flowing through your body. It keeps love pulsating through your world, touching all those you encounter. I wish you could focus on the strong core housed behind the muffin-top bulge. That core causes you to stand strong in the face of adversity. I wish you could focus on all the things, both physically and metaphorically, your cellulite laden legs have carried. I wish you could focus on every second of joy that caused the laugh-lines and every second of worried suspension that you survived that caused the forehead creases. I wish you could remember that your body is a walking universe *rivaling the wonders captured by Hubble.*

"More than your physical beauty, though, is the beauty of your soul. The soul that offers an expansive, loving acceptance of others. The soul who hurts when others hurt and feels the heaviness of not always having the needed solutions. The soul who heals with words and hugs. The soul who thinks the best about other people and who whole-heartedly believes in their potential. The soul who would never want others to look at themselves the way you more often than not look at yourself. The soul who wants everyone else to know how lovely he or she is. The soul who recognizes and sees the loveliness in others, but forgets it's her own loveliness she is projecting on everyone else.

"Would you please remember that, if you don't remember anything else I've said? You are so very lovely. Please believe that with a ferocious certainty.

"One last thing. All the little whispered longings that you keep shushing. Yes, you know the ones I'm talking about. Those whispers will become primal screams to get your attention, if you don't pay attention to them now. You can't keep telling yourself that your desires don't matter or are unimportant compared to everyone else's needs. Please stop telling your desires to take a number. You are longing for a reason. Quit pretending that those reasons aren't important. Quit pretending that you aren't important.

"My dear friend, the sum of all that you are is precious and

perfect. And I hope that all I've said will remind you of that. I hope the words will cause you to both inwardly and outwardly give yourself a long overdue benediction of love and acceptance. Why not consume yourself with self-love like you consume everything else with your beautiful love? Why not?"

I stopped talking, turned around, and walked away from my friend staring at me in the mirror.

I'm thankful that I don't have these kinds of conversations with myself anymore. At least not very often. I still have insecurities. I still get disappointed with myself regarding the way I handle situations or react to life. But there is an underlying gentleness with myself now that stems from my newfound acceptance and love for myself. And guess who that spills over to? Naturally, other people.

To love your neighbor as yourself is a basic tenet of life. We love others the way we love ourselves. That's why self-love is so important. It will change everything in your life and in the lives of others.

In his short book, *Love Yourself Like Your Life Depends on It*, Kamal Ravikant said, "The truth is to love yourself with the same intensity you would use to pull yourself up if you were hanging off a cliff with your fingers. As if your life depended on it." Because all of life does indeed, depend on love.

My niece ended a text to me recently with the words, "I love you big." I got a kick out of reading that. I thought, "Yes! We should all simply love each other big." Let's start doing that. Let's start loving each other and ourselves big.

I pray that if you don't already, you will open your heart in the deepest way to receive God's unconditional love, which will lead to you loving yourself unconditionally. May all the time you wasted questioning God's love be redeemed. May a child-like acceptance replace your skepticism and uncertainty. May wounds induced by not receiving enough love or perceiving enough love heal and be replaced by new life coming forth from all areas of your life mentally, physically, emotionally, and spiritually. Bottom line, I pray that you will be overwhelmed with love, causing your heart to radiate with light.

Remember God is Sovereign

In this chapter I want to grab your hand, so to speak, and lead you through the door labeled "Everything Else You Ever Wanted to Know about God" so we can learn more about the sovereignty of God. Or as E.E. Cummings said, "There is a hell of a good universe next door, let's go." Put on your sense of wonder and let's explore God's vastness. I'll be a guide for those who don't remember how vast God is. Because once you see a glimpse of His vastness, you'll see a glimpse of His sovereignty. And once you see a glimpse of His sovereignty, you'll learn to relax, at least somewhat, and be more lighthearted. As my Jewish friends have taught me, our anchoring certainty lies in remembering that God is sovereign; that He is in control of everything, and everything that He does is for our good. Knowing this down to the depths of our being is a key to being lighthearted.

Did you know that some Jews, who are very spiritual and learned, apologize to God every day? They apologize for how they perceived God yesterday because they realize their perception wasn't remotely close to Who and What He is. I love that. It's a humbling reminder that no matter how spiritual we are, no matter how many hours we've studied the Bible, no matter how long we've known God, or no matter how sophisticated or intellectual we are, we still haven't scratched the surface of Who and What God is. I believe that we arrive at a very good place when we cross the chasm of intellect into the realm of wonderment of God's magnificence. When we cross over into the realm of His magnificence, our doctrines, words, and opinions about Him seem somewhat foolish.

Nobel laureate physicist, Dr. Frank Wilczek said, "I came to think that if God exists, He (or She, or They, or It) did a much more impressive job revealing Himself in the world than in the old books." Another way that idea is expressed is in Psalm 19:1 when David said, "The heavens reveal the glory of God, and the sky tells of the work of His hands."

I love how God reveals Himself through nature, science, music, art, etc. God wears the world like a garment. Space, the oceans, our bodies, quantum physics, mathematics, music; these are all cloaks that God dons enabling us to see, hear, and understand aspects of Him. As Sarah Yehudit Schneider said, "God is the point of eternity that lies within each moment and each object; that which preceded creation, permeates creation, and will endure beyond its passing." Simply put, God is found anywhere and everywhere in the universe. Advancements in technology, new instruments of discovery like Hubble and powerful microscopes, new songs composed, new art created, or new equations formulated all reveal more of God. If you have access to the internet, take a minute and choose one or all of the following subjects to search. If you do, you will see and hear God.

Top and/or Amazing Hubble Images

Amazing Deep Sea Creature Images

The Spooky Actions of Entangled Particles

The Golden Ratio in Nature Images

BBC-Earth, Life Story - Courtship - Puffer Fish

Stevie Ray Vaughn's Version of *Little Wing*

Luciano Pavarotti's version of *Nessun Dorma*

In a short video entitled *Reconciling Science with Religion*, Mayim Bialik describes how she connects to God via her faith and her love and understanding of science. She says, "Understanding equations that describe gravity, pressure, force, and torque is science and that's amazing. But having a spiritual connection with that information, so much so that it brings you to your knees because it is so unbelievable, is what it means to have a relationship with God."

Bialik captures perfectly how I feel about connecting to God. Not only am I brought to my knees in awe and gratefulness for God's grace, love, mercy, and His interaction with me, but also by His intellect and creativity revealed throughout the universe. Kahlil Gibran described this kind of connection to God as "a wonder and a surprise ever springing in the soul, even while the hands hew the stone or tend the loom." And the ever springing wonder and surprise in my soul is the basis of my dependence and belief in God's sovereignty.

Albert Einstein once asked, "Do you remember how electrical currents and 'unseen waves' were laughed at? The knowledge about man is still in its infancy?" If Einstein considered the knowledge about man being in early stages, consider how much more the knowledge about God is in its infancy. Yet, even the infinitesimal understanding that I have of God helps my perspective about life. When I step back and look at all He has done and continues to do in the universe, I have to somewhat laugh at myself for doubting and worrying that He isn't "handling" things in my life.

The grandeur and precision of the universe constantly remind me that God is in control of everything. Nothing happens unless He allows it to happen. If He is completely sovereign, then that is an absolute truth. I find that truth both comforting and discomforting, though. Comforting that the One Who keeps the entire universe in order is interested enough and takes the time to keep my life in order. Yet, discomforting and confusing that this great Being of order and love allows bad things to happen.

So I need to emphasize that even though I believe in

God's sovereignty 100%, I do not understand it. And I thrive on understanding. Crave it. Search for it. Need it. But I don't often have it. Instead, I have faith. I have faith that God is sovereign, but I often lack understanding of why things happen.

His sovereignty is an anchor in my life. The first time I really had to depend on this anchor is when I had a miscarriage. Although I had been through some hard times in my life - the type of hard times that come with the territory of simply being a human - I had not suffered anything I would categorize as devastating. Having a miscarriage felt devastating. It was my first pregnancy. In addition to feeling a deep sense of loss, I worried that perhaps I wouldn't ever be able to have children. Thankfully, that wasn't the case, and I was able to carry to term two healthy babies. But I took the loss of my first baby hard.

However, what brought me comfort, but was also a source of confusion, was that God allowed the miscarriage. I didn't understand why He allowed it to happen. But I can't describe what a deep comfort it was knowing that regardless of whether I liked or understood why it happened, God was in control of my life.

Two meal-time prayers constantly remind me of God's sovereignty. Before I eat I pray, "Blessed are You, O Lord our God, Who brings forth everything by His word." Or if the meal includes bread, I pray, "Blessed are you, O Lord our God, Who brings forth bread from the earth." These simple prayers remind me that everything in life is brought forth by God. The prayers represent a dichotomy though. For instance, regarding God bringing forth the bread, obviously, God's life force caused a seed to grow into wheat. But man planted the seed, man harvested the wheat, man took the wheat to a processing plant, man turned the wheat into flour, man made the batches of bread, man packaged the bread, man delivered the bread to a store, and man operated the store where the bread was sold. Yet, I'm solely thanking God for bringing forth the bread, despite the fact that many people were involved in laborious processes in order for the bread to reach my table. The prayers are reminders that no matter how much man does, it is God Who allows and enables everything to happen.

Perhaps it's just semantics when people argue that God doesn't cause bad things to happen. Okay, maybe He doesn't cause things that we perceive as bad to happen, but He allows those things to happen. Nothing happens in this world that He doesn't allow. Logically speaking, He's either fully sovereign or He's not sovereign at all. And if He is sovereign, then He is culpable for events that happen in this world.

In the Book of Job, whatever circumstances Satan, the adversary, wanted to test/vex Job with, had to be approved by God. Which brings up a side note - there is no opposing force/entity equal to God. No force even comes close. All forces are His agents who can't do anything without His approval. Isaiah 45:7 says, "He Who forms light and creates darkness, Who makes peace and creates evil; I am the Lord, Who makes all these."

I know, I know. I do not like believing this. I do not like what it implies. I could not sit face-to-face and discuss this issue with a parent who has lost a child, with someone who has been abused, with someone who has been forced into sex trafficking, with someone who suffered the evil of the Holocaust or lost loved ones in it, or anyone who has endured a horrific tragedy. But the fact that I can't always easily talk about God's sovereignty doesn't change the fact that I believe in it.

The Jewish Mourner's Kaddish prayer, recited after the death of a close relative, is an affirmation that life still goes on even though God has just taken a human from this world. The prayer affirms that God is still exalted and good in the world that He created and operates "according to plan." That sounds harsh but necessary. As the Book of Job says, "Though He slay me, yet will I trust in Him."

I think people who have endured tragedies, yet still

believe in or have a relationship with God, are extremely brave. I recently read a comment by a man whose son was murdered by a terrorist. The murder happened years ago, but one could tell the father's pain had not diminished. His comment regarding the loss of his son was, "I still believe in God. But I will never forgive Him."

How did you react to that? Did you recoil? Judge? Understand? Pity? It doesn't really matter how we feel about the statement. What matters most is that God is big enough to handle those kinds of feelings from us. He is big enough, strong enough, and understanding enough to handle our human reactions to His infinite ways. He does not cause everything, but He allows everything. Again, comforting, but at times very, *very* confusing.

Lately, I've started praying a particular prayer for people who are going through difficult times. I pray that they will have "Song of the Sea" moments. For friends who have a child suffering from a life-threatening disease, friends watching their beloved spouses dying from diseases, friends who have lost loved ones in unexpected accidents, friends who are under the constant threat of terrorist attacks; so many people I know and love are in the midst of extremely hard, on-going circumstances.

A "Song of the Sea" moment is what collective Israel experienced after crossing the Red Sea. Every person, from the lowliest servant to Miriam, Moses, and Aaron, clearly understood that all the hardships of enslavement in Egypt were Divinely orchestrated. Linear time dissolved and they saw how their hardships fit into a Divine plan leading to redemption. For a few moments, they were all-knowing prophets who understood how everything worked together for their good. "Song of the Sea" moments are gifts of certainty and clarity that transcend time during difficulty, ensuring us that God is orchestrating everything in our lives for our ultimate good, even when it does not feel good.

Certainty, clarity, and transcendence come to me when I go out at night and look at the stars. I become reoriented. Besides being so beautiful, the stars are a powerful reminder that despite how small my life is, the Creator of all that I am beholding is kind enough to take the time to be directly involved in my life. And even though I often don't understand His ways, I am assured that everything that happens is a part of His plan and is for my ultimate good. Abraham Joshua Heschel captured the essence of this type of moment when he wrote, "We can never sneer at the stars, mock the dawn or scoff at the totality of being . . . Away from the immense, cloistered in our own concepts, we may scorn or revile everything. But standing between earth and sky, we are silenced by the sight."

Sometimes no prayer is as powerful, nor moment so clear,

than when standing in silence at the sight of God. And during the silence, His sovereignty transcends words, thoughts, and beliefs and slips into the depths of our being with a gentle force that pushes reason aside and replaces it with ancient knowing that He is. He just is. And that is everything.

Thank you, God, for bringing us to moments of awed silence when Your ineffable vastness, grandeur, and sovereignty are revealed to us in increments that literally take our breath, our worries, and our words away. I pray that we will continue to have our hearts, minds, and eyes wide open to Your vastness, grandeur, and sovereignty. May our finite minds find rest in Your infiniteness. I pray that we would trust You even when we don't understand You and that during the uncertainties of our lives we would have certainty that You are good and do good, even when it doesn't feel good.

Remember the Kingdom

In the previous chapter, I reminded you of God's sovereignty. In this chapter, I will remind you about His Kingdom. This world, which is part of His Kingdom, was created as a place for us to thrive. Yet, we sometimes feel lost in this world and feel like we are withering rather than thriving. At other times, though, we have periods of exponential growth like the man described in Psalm 1:3 who is like "a tree by streams of living water bearing its fruit in season, whose leaves never wither. Everything he does prospers." Whichever category we currently fit into, I think it will be beneficial to us to remember a few basic tenets about the Kingdom.

People of varying faiths believe that the Kingdom of Heaven can be experienced on earth. Does that mean that they believe a Kingdom is going to fall out of the sky? No, it means that they believe that if we think and act according to how God set up the operational system of His Kingdom, we will experience Heaven on earth. I believe this, too, or at least believe that we can experience a great amount of the Kingdom of Heaven on earth.

There is so much more to our lives and the Kingdom than

meets our eyes. The Kingdom is a vast, infinite concept. God is incorporeal, but to help us understand His Kingdom, imagine this: Imagine God with His chest wide open. Imagine Him beckoning us to step inside of Him to a place that has more love, peace, happiness, and wholeness than we've ever dreamt of. That is the Kingdom. The Kingdom is God. It is all of Him.

Obviously, we can't really step inside of God, right? Or can we? I believe that we can. And the way we step inside is with our minds. Dr. Frank Wilczek said about physics, "I invite you to expand your view of reality. Advancements require adjustments and expansions of our perception of reality." I invite you to do the same. To adjust and expand your perceptions about the Kingdom of Heaven and how we experience it through our mindsets.

God, who is obviously the King of the Kingdom, is sometimes referred to in certain religious/mystical practices as "The Upper Force." As mentioned earlier, the names I call the King/Upper Force are God, Universe, and Source. The King/Upper Force rules over everything, including us, His subjects. But the way in which He rules, or exerts His Upper Force, is often misunderstood. So let's remember what the Kingdom is like.

The first tenet is what I wrote about in the chapter "Remember to Love Yourself." This basic tenet of the

Kingdom, that will vastly improve our lives if we firmly establish it in our minds, is that God loves us more than we could ever imagine. Think about the love you feel for someone. Now multiply that love by the highest number possible (which is infinite). God's love is exactly like Him; endless. We are the ones who make His love quantitative. It's tragic that we do so. Do you really think that God expects us to love Him with all of our heart, soul, and minds - in other words, with our entire being - without Him reciprocating that kind of love? God loves us with His entire being. What an incredible gift that, sadly, many of us don't receive. It doesn't matter how much God loves us if we don't believe that He loves us. The Kingdom reflects our beliefs and feelings. If you think that God doesn't love you, then that is what is going to be reflected back to you. It's not because God doesn't love you. It's because you experience what you believe is there for you. I've chosen to believe that God's love for me is endless. And that is exactly what I'll experience. Endless love.

Another tenet of the Kingdom is that God created this world for us and that it is for pleasure rather than for suffering. More and more people are escaping the collective belief that mankind is relegated to suffering. Escaping this collective consciousness of suffering can sometimes be like trying to escape quicksand, though. It seems impossible.

I love studying and reading about history, at least part of me does. I'm fascinated by history, but I can't seem to finish any books about history that I start. I've started books about World War I and II, the rise of communism in Russia and China, and the conflicts in the Middle East, but I can't make it to the end of the books because I find the suffering throughout these historical accounts so depressing. It seems like history is synonymous with suffering.

I greatly admire people who are living in war-torn countries or under conditions where they don't have basic freedoms and necessities, but can somehow still believe that the world was not created for suffering. It's much easier to believe that we aren't meant to suffer when we have sufficient food and shelter and when we aren't in constant fear for our lives. I'm not marginalizing suffering, and I certainly don't know how to explain suffering. The thought of people suffering throughout the world keeps me awake at night, as I'm sure it does others. But the suffering I see doesn't keep me from believing that this world is made for our pleasure and I want to receive as much pleasure as possible.

I don't think it's shallow to want to experience pleasure. How do you feel when you see the ocean or one of your favorite places in nature? My eyes can't drink in the sight of the ocean enough. I can't take enough deep breaths of the ocean air. Anytime I'm at the beach I have to pull myself away when leaving because of the pleasure I feel when I'm there. I feel the same way, maybe even more so, about being at an MLB baseball game. My eyes can't take in the sight enough (because I happen to think that the combination of baseball parks, baseball fields under the bright lights, and baseball uniforms are one of the prettiest sights in the world). My ears can't take in the sound of the bat hitting the ball enough. I love everything about baseball games. My heart is full of pleasure when I'm at one. And every pleasure that I experience in life turns into praise and thankfulness to God for letting me experience such a moment.

I love this world that was created for me and I want to experience the pleasure of it as much as possible. Humans are programmed to pursue pleasure. But what differentiates us from other creatures is our ability to not just pursue physical pleasure, but spiritual pleasure, too. We will never be completely happy unless we have a desire for spiritual pleasures and act upon those desires in a balanced way. Mindfulness to pursue knowing God, giving charity to the poor, helping people, encouraging people, using our talents to bring beauty into the world, doing justice, etc., all of these are ways of experiencing pleasure both physically and spiritually.

Often we tend to compartmentalize our spirituality. But I

love letting spirituality spill over into every area of my life. Yet, vice versa, too. I love letting the physical aspects of life spill over into my spirituality. The intermingling of the spiritual and physical makes life more fun, more meaningful, and more purposeful. I love finding God and experiencing God at a baseball game as much as I love finding Him in a religious text or in a quiet, meditative moment. As Elizabeth Barrett Browning wrote, "Natural things and spiritual - who separates those two in art, in morals, or the social drift tears up the bond of nature and brings death." The pursuit of pleasure in this world with mindfulness and soulfulness and the bonding between the physical and spiritual infuses us with life.

I understand that sometimes we tend to cry out to God more or seek Him more purposefully in the midst of suffering. But I challenge us to cry out to Him in joyful exclamation as we connect to Him purposefully during the "ordinary" day-to-day moments in our lives and also in the fun I-can't-believe-I'm-getting-to-do-this moments of our lives. If joy and thanksgiving break through constrictions more than tears, (as will be discussed in the chapter "Remember to be Happy,") then maybe it's time to make *tikkun* (repairs in this world) through the vehicle of pleasure rather than through suffering.

For some, it will require a big leap of faith and a paradigm shift to stop believing that we were made for suffering more than for pleasure. Psalm 40 describes how God pulls us out of a "slimy pit and thick mud and mire" to "firmly establish our feet upon a rock." I think this is an apt picture of how He can pull us out of the collective consciousness of expecting to suffer. And then He can help us firmly establish in our minds that this world was made for pleasure.

The Kingdom also operates on the tenet that God wants and does only good for us. If we can grasp this concept it will enhance our lives by giving us peace despite not always understanding why things happen. Do you have trust issues with God? Ask Him to help you believe that He is good and only wants and does good for you and I guarantee that you will become more peaceful. Believing that God wants only good for us will help us relax in the midst of problems that we are facing. It might not make our situations any easier, but the assurance that life is happening for us and for our good will bring a calmness to our hearts and minds.

Life really is happening for us, not to us. I know that can be hard to hear sometimes, especially if we are prone to think of ourselves as victims. And what can be even harder to hear is that we are co-creating all that is happening to us. We are co-creators, via our free-will, with God. Being a co-creator concerns me sometimes because I make mistakes.

God is trying to create wonderful things in my life, yet He's got me as a partner. I find myself praying, or really begging, "Please help me do my part of co-creating better." And you know what? God always helps me in spite of myself.

We are going to make mistakes. That is a given. Making mistakes is part of the human condition. But after each mistake we make, God recalibrates our path. I think at times we trust a GPS navigation system more than we trust God. God is for us. He desires for us to fulfill our purposes in life and to reach our destinations that He has planned for us even more than we desire that for ourselves. So when we make a wrong turn He doesn't flag us down, yell "Stop the car!," ask us to hand over the keys, and leave us stranded on the highway of life. Instead, He helps us reroute in order to get back on the intended course.

King David's humanity was very extreme. Jewish sages teach that he experienced every emotion a person is capable of experiencing. The Psalms he wrote resonate with the complexities of being human. His musings, questions, supplications, and thanksgivings literally represent the highs and lows of being human.

God is not appalled by our humanity. Nor is He surprised when we make mistakes or fall. He is so happy for us when we decide to pick ourselves up and keep going despite our mistakes. We are humans in a spiritual Kingdom. That is a setup for inevitable complications and conflicts. That's why God is patient with us and slow to anger; He remembers that we are made of dust. And that's why He sends us constant help. He always wants what's best for us as we navigate our way in this Kingdom of duality: The duality of God being within us, yet everywhere around us. The duality of God allowing the illusion of separateness, yet we are always connected to Him and each other. The duality of God often seeming hidden, yet He is always with us. The duality of the physical world seeming more important and real than the unseen world, yet the physical world is only a branch of the tree and roots of the spiritual, unseen world. Bottom line, it takes a great amount of faith to live in this Kingdom of duality as physical/spiritual beings. Yet, at the same time, it is what we were made for.

Another basic tenet of the Kingdom is that our thoughts and attitudes are powerful tools of creation. They play a vital role in determining the quality of our lives. If our thoughts are always negative and we have bad attitudes, this negativity will be reflected in our lives. For example, if we think that people are mean and annoying, we will continuously encounter people who we perceive as mean and annoying. If we think that life is always a battle, we will continuously have conflict.

The good news is that the opposite is true. If we think

that people are kind, good, and want to help us, we will continuously encounter people who we perceive as kind, good, and who want to help us. If we think that life is fabulous, fabulous events will occur in our lives. Our thoughts constantly attract back to us the energy and expectations that we emit.

A Jewish adage is to "think good, and it will be good." The Lubavitcher Rebbe expounded on this connection to *bitachon*, which is absolute trust in God. *Bitachon* is a powerful feeling of optimism based not on reason or experience, but based on faith that God is magnanimous, that He is good and does only good. The Lubavitcher Rebbe said that when we trust in God by thinking that things will be good, we become conduits, like lightening rods, which draw down and receive revealed blessings of good. In this line of reasoning, positive thoughts attract positive events. By feeling blessed, we actually attract blessings.

One day when I was checking out at the grocery store, the clerk ask me what my summer plans were. I told him that my daughter and I were taking a trip to New York City to celebrate her graduation. He immediately went into a negative mode and commented on how rude he thought the people in NYC were. I gave him a surprised look and said, "When I went a few years ago I thought the New Yorkers were the nicest people in the world. I loved being around them." He seemed just as surprised by my answer. I got what I expected when I was in NYC. I believe people are nice and helpful. And they were. My sisters, parents, and I still talk about our "angel" in a suit and with a briefcase who we encountered in the subway tunnel. He saw how confused we were trying to decide which tickets we needed to purchase to get to the Bronx for a Yankees game. He took our money, purchased our tickets, and practically held our hands as he herded us to ensure that we got on the right train just in time. His kindness immensely touched us and helped us. My family and I are habitually kind to people. So it's no surprise that we draw kindness back into our lives.

We are made in the image of God. We are consciousness, as He is, but unlike Him, we operate in the form of a body. But don't let being in a body fool you into believing that our thoughts aren't powerful. They direct energy and draw energy back to us. They create what we experience in the physical dimension. We are walking communication command centers sending out signals all the time. And the signals that we consistently send out form our reality. As a man thinks, so he is. We should do ourselves a favor and stop thinking detrimental thoughts and stop thinking the worst all of the time. Instead, we should risk having positive expectations along with positive actions. Because another basic tenet of the Kingdom is a simple equation: Good thoughts + Actions = Magic.

I'm human, so of course, I think negatively sometimes. At times I even have a propensity to get melancholy about hard situations that my loved ones or people around the world are experiencing, or that I'm experiencing. I'm an INFJ personality type and a moon child. Short translation: whatever I feel, I feel it *very* deeply. So I work hard to guard my thoughts. When I'm a proficient guardian, my thoughts are very positive. If I'm a slacker instead, well, let's just say my thoughts can get rather grim.

When the people I love in Israel are experiencing extremely difficult circumstances, my father will call me to check on me and say, "You can't let it get you down for too long. You've got to stay positive, especially so your kids won't see you get too down." His advice echoed that of a trusted mentor, who lives in Israel, who once chided me for getting so melancholy about the tragic events happening throughout the world, and especially in Israel. He said, "We have neither the time nor luxury to dwell on negative thoughts. There's too much else for us to do." It was his way of saying, "Suck it up, Buttercup!"

Events in life will make us sad. Maybe even despondent at times. But we aren't designed to perpetually stay in a sad or negative frame of mind. There's too much for us to do in this wonderful world for us to be sad or negative all of the time. But I don't say that lightly. Many people suffer from clinical depression. I pray that if you are suffering from depression that you will get the exact kind of help that you need, and that you will be able to be lighthearted again. I pray that you will be able to take off the spirit of heaviness and instead wear a garment of lightheartedness.

A few years ago, my father gave me a decorative key ring with large old-fashioned keys on it to remind me that I hold the keys to the Kingdom in my hands. Imagine that I am handing you a set, too. As you look at and handle each key and hear them clank against each other, remember what they represent. Each key represents a frame of mind that will help you operate optimally and with lightheartedness as you experience the Kingdom of Heaven on earth through your thoughts and beliefs:

Key 1: God loves us.

Key 2: The world was created for pleasure, not for suffering.

Key 3: God wants only good for us.

Key 4: Life is happening for us, not to us.

Key 5: We are co-creators with God.

Key 6: We will make mistakes. But God will recalibrate and reroute our paths.

Key 7: Our thoughts create our reality. Think good, and it will be good.

Bonus Key 8: Life is good. And it's going to get even better. Really.

I pray that if we are in a negative frame of mind that we will adjust our mindsets as easily as a radio channel is adjusted. If we are on "stations" of untruths, detrimental beliefs, pessimism, and low expectations, I pray that we will change our "stations" to truths, healthy beliefs, optimism, and great expectations. Help us, God, open our hearts and minds in the deepest way to Your infinite love. Let that love saturate us and spill over into everything we do and believe. I pray that our partnership with You as co-creators will be so beneficial to the world. If we are in a victim mode, help us break out of it and relish the fact that life is happening for us as we co-create with You. When we make mistakes, help us learn from them as we get up and keep living with determination and faith. Lastly, please help us relax. You know that we have desires that we desperately want fulfilled. But help us relax in the fact that what we want to happen doesn't happen until it happens, or maybe something even better will happen, instead. Help us trust that whatever You deem best, will happen in just the right hour. Thank You for letting us exist in Your Kingdom and may we experience, in fullness, all that we can of Your Kingdom on earth.

Remember to Receive

This chapter is hot off the presses, so to speak, because it represents an aspect of my life that I am newly implementing. I'm learning how to receive. And I love it. Not so much because of what I'm receiving, even though I love receiving things. But because of what my newfound attitude about receiving is doing for God. It's bringing Him pleasure. And there's a place in my soul that is jumping up and down about that.

Over the last two decades, my Jewish friends have taught me this foundational aspect of their faith - to pray to have the will to receive in order to bring God pleasure and to benefit others. So I knew this principle, had contemplated it, had prayed about it, had talked about it, had even taught others about it. But the truth of the principle had not seeped down into that place of my soul where I knew it in such a way that it altered my life. That seepage is finally happening and it feels fantastic.

Whether you think this is appropriate or not, or think it's the weirdest thing you've ever read, I'm going to go ahead and just say it . . . the best analogy, in my opinion, of learning to have the will to receive is when a couple makes love. Before you toss the book aside, I mean that in the sincerest way. Sex is holy and is incredible. And it is an apt analogy of how the physical dimension mirrors a profound aspect of the spiritual dimension between God and man. The connection between a couple when they have sex is a picture of the connection God wants to have with humans on a spiritual/soul level. He wants that kind of closeness with us. Our deepest longings mirror God's longing for us. The profound writings of Abraham Joshua Heschel remind us that God is always in search of man. He said, "It is as if I were the only man on the globe and God, too, were alone, waiting for me."

Backing up just a bit . . . all the way back to the Garden of Eden, man and woman were created in the image of God. On a very elementary level, part of what that represents is that God, Who has no form and is above gender, still has both male and female characteristics. The two physical forms - male and female - act as a living metaphor for the two ways in which God makes His presence known. When the energy of God interacts with mankind in a masculine way, God's names representing those aspects of Him are in the masculine grammatical form. When the energy of God interacts with mankind in a feminine way, God's names representing those aspects of "Him" are in the feminine grammatical form. (Hebrew belongs to a group of languages in which words have a grammatical gender.) For example, the aspect of God known as the Divine Presence, that we feel inside of us as nurturing and comforting, is known by the name *Shechinah*, which is a feminine word. For the most part, though, God's energy interacting with us is masculine because most often He is giving to us. He is the Bestower. And that brings us back to the point I opened this chapter with of having the will to receive in order to bring God pleasure and to benefit others.

I grew up hearing teachings about desiring to be blessed so I could, in turn, be a blessing to others. I am surrounded by family and friends who do this; who are walking examples of being blessed in order to be a blessing. They are the most generous people. It's a beautiful cycle to behold. They literally are paying forward the blessings they receive from God. They embody the part of the prayer that asks for "the will to receive in order to benefit others."

The part of the prayer that is seeping into my soul is "to bring God pleasure." It's such a profound aspect of our relationship with God. And it is literally making my heart radiate with light knowing that the act of receiving from Him brings Him pleasure.

God loves to give. Giving is His nature. He cannot, not give. He is the Great Benefactor. He is Source and Source is always flowing and always giving.

God created us to be vessels to receive Him; to receive Source. Judaism has a deep, beautiful concept (called *tzimtzum*) regarding the reason why and how God, Who is everything, Who is all, constricted Himself just enough to enable room for conceptual space to exist - hence the universe came into existence. And out of the entire universe comes you - a vessel; the number one, most desired place God wants His Source to flow into. Look around you at this beautiful planet and the rest of the universe that surrounds us. God's energy, His Source, flows into everything and sustains everything. A blade of grass growing. A ray of sunshine beaming down. The courses of the planets. A bird flying. A thunderstorm forming. All of these things have His life force flowing through them. But you are unique in the way that you are able to respond to receiving His life force. He created you so that He could experience the pleasure of giving to a vessel who wanted, loved, and allowed themselves to receive from Him and who responded with thankfulness and pleasure. What has hit me smack in the heart is how much He loves my response to His giving.

For instance, I love eating. I mean I really, *really* love food. Sometimes I'll take a bite of something that tastes so exceptionally good and as I relish it I think, "I can't believe how good this is." But do you know who I'm saying that to? Not just myself. I'm saying that to God. First of all, it was so nice of Him to make food have a taste. He could have made food bland or made everything taste the same. The concept of taste is incredible to me. And the fact that God created so much variety regarding taste is such a nice thing that He did for us. So I don't just thank Him for food. I also let Him know how much I enjoy eating it. Not only because it literally sustains my life, which I love living, but because it's so pleasurable to taste.

I find myself reacting to life more and more in this way. I just want Him to know how much I love receiving from Him. When my eyes see a beautiful sunset, landscape or person; when my ears hear a beautiful song or laughter; when my nose smells a lovely scent; when my brain thinks deep thoughts or processes funny jokes; when my heart feels love or gratitude; when I watch a sporting event; I let Him know how deeply grateful I am to be on the receiving end of these different facets of His never-ending Source. And to be honest, even when I am going through painful, uncomfortable, this-is-not-what-I-wanted moments, I thank Him too, because He is the sovereign Source of all that I am experiencing.

Bottom line, I am learning to receive to bring Him pleasure. I'm learning to be a vessel who wants to remove any blockages I might have in my life so I can receive as much of Him as possible. I'm a visual person, so sometimes

I picture myself aligned with Him like the Space Shuttle aligned and synced itself with the International Space Station when docking. I want that kind of precise alignment and syncing of my life with Him. So I think these kinds of thoughts as I pray to help me open and align my life to all He has for me. Because when I am in that place of alignment, which I hope to perpetually be in, I am a conduit of His Source of blessings, not just for myself, but for others, too. This source of abundance from Him is known as *shefa*.

"You open Your hand and satisfy the desires of every living thing." Psalm 145:16 gives us a beautiful picture of God's constant, never-run-out-of *shefa* that is always flowing to us. Bestowal, known as the unchanging "Thought of Creation," is the foundation of creation. The main essence of the "Thought of Creation" is God's desire to do good to all He creates. This is one reason the universe continues to expand. Once creation was enacted - once Source started flowing - it could never stop. There is no edge or end to the universe. It extends infinitely and continually because it's an extension of Source, of infinite bestowal. Found throughout nature and in our own bodies is beautiful, perfectly encoded energy by the Creator that sets expansion and growth into motion continuously. This incredible Source is what continuously wants to flow through us and give things to us.

Think about why you want things. Is it solely for selfish

reasons? For power over people? For control of people? To feed lusts and greed? So you can be "better" than others? So you'll feel secure? So you'll feel happy?

What if we wanted things and got the biggest kick out of receiving things, but not just because we got what we wanted, but because we looked beyond getting our desires met and looked to the Source Who fulfilled our desires? What if our gratitude matched or exceeded our excitement of getting what we wanted?

The highest, most evolved place we can ascend to is a place of selfless receiving. A place where altruism replaces egoism. A place where doubt of whether we deserve to receive is replaced with the pure joy and assurance of being a human vessel who was created to bring pleasure to God by receiving from Him. By opening ourselves to receive from Him, we simultaneously become givers to Him. That is an amazing vis-à-vis.

I pray that you will have the will to receive in order to bring God pleasure and to benefit others. May you experience a beautiful alignment, syncing and docking with Source and open yourself - heart, mind, and soul - to receive His *shefa* (never ending abundance). And may His *shefa* brim and spill over from you to bring comfort, care, and delights to those around you. I pray that your heart will swell with a joy you have not previously known as you learn for the first time, or learn to delve even deeper, into a place of receiving from the Creator to bring Him pleasure.

Remember to Heal Yourself

Please note that the advice I give in this chapter is not meant to replace advice from your health practitioners. It is meant to supplement your pathway to healing and to remind you that your natural state is wellness.

Deep down you know this, so I'm just reminding you that you are so much more than flesh and bone. You are energy. And your energy comes from a vast, infinite Source; from God. As discussed in the previous chapter, God is literally the Source of life flowing through us. That life force is unchanging and constant. We are the variable that changes.

When Source flows through us uninhibited, we feel it in our spirit, mind, and body. It's simply called feeling good. And feeling good feels good. In fact, feeling good feels great. But when Source is blocked from flowing freely through us, we don't feel as good. Little blockages = little discomforts. Big blockages = big discomforts, which often manifest as diseases. But as stated above, Source does not change, it is constant, so if we are lacking in Source it's often because we have created a blockage.

The blockages I will focus on in this chapter are emotional blockages. Because our level of lightheartedness is, in large part, determined by which emotions we allow ourselves to consistently feel and manifest. As science catches up with what spiritual and holistic healers have always known, scientific data reminds us how emotions impact our health. For example, stress and sadness can weaken the immune system. And laughter and happiness can actually strengthen the immune system. Plain and simple, our physical bodies respond to our emotions. Ever felt yourself blush? Or felt butterflies in your stomach? Ever seen someone glowing because they are in love? The mind and body are intricately connected. So, although it is not always the case, it is not uncommon that physical ailments are secondary issues of emotional ailments.

Physical ailments are one way our souls try to get our attention to tell us that we are out of balance. Sometimes we don't have to investigate very deeply for the cause of why we don't feel good due to being imbalanced. Lack of adequate rest, eating food that doesn't give us nutrients and energy, and/or long-term stress are often what leads to feeling bad, or worse to sickness and disease. But often physical ailments are an indication of an emotional issue that has caused a blockage to the flow of Source.

If we hang on to negative emotions for too long, they become like a damn blocking the flow of Source. In *The Body Mind Workbook*, Debbi Shapiro explains, "It is not a quick and soon forgotten flash of anger or despair that will set off the alarm system (from the cerebral cortex). It is the cumulative effect of constant or long-repressed negative emotions that will do it. The longer the unacknowledged state of mind is maintained, the more damage it can do as it wears down the body/mind resistance and constantly gives out a negative life message."

We might easily be able to tell someone, "I have such-and-such disease." But how easy would it be for us to say, "I haven't been able to forgive so-and-so for years and that unforgiveness is manifesting itself in my stomach"? I know that might sound weird or even ignorant to some people. But our physical condition is a barometer of our emotional condition. For instance, some of you would easily be able to answer these kinds of questions while others would think I was crazy for asking them:

Q: When one has not been able to let go of grief, where does this usually manifest physically?

A: The lungs.

Q: What body part is the seat of anger?

A.The liver.

Q. What body part does perpetual fear tend to manifest itself outwardly?

A: The knees.

If we only view life through a Western mindset we tend to

forget that there are reasons that we don't feel good beyond the fact that "we just don't feel good." How much soul investigating do you do when you don't feel good? If God forbid, you were diagnosed with a disease, would you only look for a physical cure, or would you be prone to also look further inward at your soul's condition and at your connection to Source?

Our perpetual positive or negative emotional state will manifest itself as either vibrant health or as acute sickness or chronic disease. Psalm 41:5 is a succinct, yet powerful verse that I pray for myself and others when praying for healing. It says, "Heal my soul, Lord, and I will be healed." That is what we need help with; healing our souls. The Jewish prayer for healing recognizes the body/soul connection when it says, "May it be Your will that You speedily send a complete recovery from Heaven, a healing of the body and a healing of the spirit."

Please don't feel guilty or feel like you've done something wrong if you are dealing with a disease. Just begin to look at the disease differently. Your disease is not a separate entity. It is not something you are "fighting." Hear me out. It is actually part of your body, a part of you. If you can see it this way, and acknowledge your body's current condition as being a part of you, without welcoming the disease to stay, it will make all the difference in the world. Your body brought you a message that you might not have heard another way. Thank your body for bringing the message, but then tell it that it no longer has to be in a diseased state. It has done its "job" of getting your attention and can now go back to being in its natural state of wellness.

We are designed to feel good. Don't let yourself believe otherwise. And we are encoded with an innate capability to heal. Each spring bluebonnets that my grandmother planted decades ago start blooming in my yard. They are perennials that are encoded by Source to come back each year. Yet, even though they are encoded to grow each year, they require certain elements like sunlight, water, and soil for their growth. Our bodies are the same way. We are encoded to grow and heal, but our bodies require certain elements, including emotional well-being, for growth and healing to occur.

As touched on in another chapter, even though some religions and spiritual disciplines believe in and teach that that the world is made for suffering and that we most likely will be and/or should be suffering, that is not true. Yes, we obviously will go through times of suffering, but we don't have to perpetually suffer. One of the reasons that we do suffer, though, is when Source isn't flowing through us.

We are energy in motion. A simplistic break down, but one that might help us understand ourselves better is to see the word "emotion" as e-motion; energy in motion. Which e-motions flow through us freely and cause us to feel good? Of course that's an easy answer. Positive e-motions. And it's just as easy to see how negative e-motions don't move through us as freely. Ironically, even though negative e-motions don't feel good, they are the ones we tend to hold on to or bury deep within. Often we have to coax ourselves or be coaxed by trusted family or friends, or by a counselor or spiritual mentor to let go of anger, unforgiveness, hatred, jealousy, fear, obsessiveness, etc.

As you remember to see yourself as energy, you will naturally start recognizing which emotions, foods, people, places, spiritual practices, exercises, amounts of sleep, songs, activities, etc., tend to make you feel as if Source is freely flowing through you or is blocked.

(Let me pause and give some of you a loving smack on the forehead. You know who you are, the ones who do it all. I mean *all*. You are amazing, but you never slow down enough to take care of yourself, much less take the time to recharge. You pay more attention to your cell phone than you pay attention to yourself. You would never consider not recharging your phone's battery or getting if fixed if it stopped working, yet you go weeks, years, sometimes decades without giving yourself what you need to recharge or to be fixed. The world needs you. So, take some time and ask these questions: Is Source freely flowing through me? If not, what is preventing the flow? What do I need to do to recharge or to get well? These are serious, vital questions to ask yourself. Then it is vital that you *act* upon the answers, which will be obvious.)

The Sea of Galilee and the Dead Sea are two beautiful bodies of water in Israel. Both are fed by the same source, the Jordan River, but only one of the bodies of water is full of life. The one full of life is the Sea of Galilee which has an outlet for its source to flow through. The Dead Sea does not have an outlet. Although it is a strangely beautiful body of water, it has no life growing in it. The lack of an outlet for its source causes an inability to sustain life.

Are you hanging on to or have you buried emotions that are inhibiting Source from flowing through you causing you to become stagnant like the Dead Sea? If you answered yes, then it's time to let go.

How do you let go? There are many ways, and as I mentioned previously, this book will be a springboard for you, propelling you to make changes. Some of you will be able to let go of negative emotions by yourself, simply with intention and perhaps prayer. Some of you might need to go to a counselor to help you know how to let issues go that you have held on to for so long or have buried deep within. Some of you might need to go to a spiritual/healing practitioner to work with you. Or you might incorporate all of these steps and others.

Whatever method that comes to you of how you should begin your process of emotional healing will be the right way, because remember, you inherently know what you need and how you need to heal. Trust your instincts on which route you need to take to help bring about your healing. As Albert Schweitzer said, "Each patient carries his own doctor inside of him."

There is a magical moment, which is the smallest time imaginable, between one moment into the next. It is the subtle moment when something has ended, but the next thing hasn't begun yet. This "between" moment is a profound anything-is-possible moment. The past is past and the future hasn't happened yet. It is a place of potential. But change requires change. We can't keep doing the same thing and expect or get change. I believe what Viktor Frankl concluded about life, is an apt description for healing, too, when he said, "Between stimulus and response there is a space. In that space is the power to choose our response. In that power lies our growth and our freedom."

There's a power of choice that lives in the subtle "between" instant when something ends and what follows hasn't begun yet. Magic and miracles are born in those moments. All possibilities still exist. From this place we are given the chance to heal, change, or continue as is.

Our bodies, our souls, our lives - have the potential to change, regenerate, and heal if we will redirect our thoughts, intentions, and actions during the "between" moments. We are given this chance, literally every second of the day, to choose life.

I was given a second chance to choose life a few years ago and did so with gusto. I go to a health practitioner who uses bio-feedback to "hear" what the body says, via electronic energetic scans and computer readouts. These readouts show in what areas the body is physically imbalanced and the requirements the body is lacking for healing to occur. Many times the scans have accurately shown conditions in my body such as hormonal imbalance, what nutrients I was lacking, or which organs were not functioning optimally. During one appointment though, the scan showed something more serious.

I won't give all the details, but I will disclose that what the scan showed, if not taken care of, was life-threatening. Guess what the first thing I did was? I went home and prayed. But not the kind of prayer you might expect. First, I told God "thank You." I knew that He was sovereign and that for some reason He was allowing this to happen. I also told Him how much I loved life and that I wanted to continue living. Then I began to address the emotional issue that this physical condition was stemming from. I had a heart-to-heart and pour-your-guts-out kind of talk with God about an issue I had pushed deep inside to "get out of the way."

I had a "Hezekiah" moment. The story of Hezekiah is recorded in the Books of Isaiah and II Kings. A prophet revealed to Hezekiah that due to sickness he had a limited amount of time to live. Upon hearing the news, Hezekiah "turned his face to the wall" and prayed for healing and an extension of life.

Hezekiah turning to face the wall was much more than a physical movement. It was an inward movement. The face he turned was his awareness, and the wall he looked at was an inward soul condition that he knew he had to address and fix to initiate his physical healing. Upon hearing the news that I was sick, that is what I immediately did. I turned my face to my wall.

I was not surprised to find out that I was sick because I knew that I was sick in my soul. Yet, even though I knew that, I had not done anything about it. I had been deeply hurt a few years prior. I knew that if I did not let go of the hurt, it would eventually cause damage to my physical body. I knew this in my head. But I still had not let the hurt go. The onset of this physical sickness was my merciful wake-up call. So I got busy. I did some intense soul work which involved forgiving those who had hurt me, but mainly involved getting back in the arena of *living* life. I had stopped living with passion. I was too busy holding up armor. Consumption with protecting myself from being hurt again was preventing me from living in fullness. So I put the heavy armor down, decided to be vulnerable again, decided to be effective again, and got back to living out my life's mission.

Again, from *The Body Mind Workbook*, Shapiro says, "The language of the body/mind is surprisingly simple to understand. Unearthing the inner conflict is the first step; dealing with that inner conflict and transforming it from conflict to resolution and peace is what enables healing to take place. It is not an easy task, however, not one that everyone will want to undertake, for it demands that we deal with all those aspects of ourselves that we have been spending years ignoring."

Please note, I took physical steps too, under the advice of my trusted health practitioner, to give my body what it needed to physically heal. But the first and foremost thing that I did was take steps to heal my soul. I knew until that was taken care of my healing would not be complete.

Thankfully, I did heal. And I became pro-active and deliberate at letting Source flow through me. But even with that kind of deliberateness and knowledge, I still need help sometimes from outside sources to remain well in my spirit, soul, and body. None of us are above needing help. As Giancarlo Stanton, an elite MLB player said regarding significant steps he took for emotional healing after the death of a close friend, "The most powerful people in the world would still need some type of healing process when something like that happens."

I bet most of you are like me in the sense that it is not easy to ask for help. One of the few times that I went to counseling the counselor said, "Do you realize that you have a habit of dismissing your needs? You literally shrug your shoulders every time you voice that you might actually need something."

I had to chuckle at that because it's true. I feel guilty for having "problems" because I'm blessed in so many other ways. (See, I can't even write the word "problems" without putting it in quotation marks.) I feel like I have to refer to my problems as #FirstWorldProblems or as a song says, "middle class and tame" problems if I refer to them at all. I've tried to stop doing that and accept the fact that I'm not above being human. Surprise, surprise. I'm a human and I have problems and needs. Granted, my problems and needs aren't as serious compared to a lot of people's problems. But still, they are my problems and needs to figure out and deal with the best that I can.

After I began my journey of healing, I started telling myself something repeatedly. My mantra became, "I am balanced and at ease." (Since being at ease is the opposite of dis-ease.) And I became what I thought. A few check-ups later, my health practitioner looked at my readout and literally said, "Wow, you are so balanced." I loved hearing that. Along with other steps that I took, my body responded to all the good things I did for it, including thinking positive thoughts, and I healed.

My story is not unique. We've all been hurt. We've all held on to or buried our hurt or negative emotions and our bodies have suffered from that decision. Yet, our bodies are waiting to be just as responsive to other, healthier decisions that we make.

Dear God, Who is our Source for everything, including healing, please help us let go of all the things we need to release. If we need to turn inward and face a wall, help us do that. Help us heal our souls through whatever avenues and ways You deem fit for our particular condition, and let it lead to physical healing. Help us become and stay balanced and at ease as You, our Source, flows freely through us.

Remember to Sit With Your Pain

Pain. It hurts. And the longer we ignore it or resist it, the longer it's going to hurt. That's why we need to sit with it. Not invite it in as a permanent guest. But at least sit with it long enough to listen to the message it is trying to tell us. I think it's safe to assume that we carry enough weight of responsibilities and concerns without carrying the weight of pain, too. To become more lighthearted, we need let go of the weight of pain. And to do that requires looking pain straight in the eyes and saying, "Have a seat."

The pain I'm addressing in this chapter is recurring and long-standing mental and emotional pain. I wavered on whether to include this chapter since it will require me to be even more vulnerable than I've been in other parts of the book. Also, this chapter could easily be misunderstood. But it's worth the risk of being vulnerable and of being misunderstood because learning to sit with pain has revolutionized my life. Maybe you need that kind of revolution, too. If so, then it's worth writing this chapter just for you.

I won't share the specific kind of emotional pain that continuously showed up in my life. I think I can get my point across without revealing the specifics. The pain I felt wasn't unique, though. And it wasn't horrible. But pain is pain, especially when you are the one dealing with it.

So even though my pain was not horrible, it still hurt. And it was a frequent visitor in my life. Sometimes it would arrive for just a fleeting visit. It would follow me around not saying a word, but letting its presence be felt loud and clear. Other times, it felt like an incessant, needy child pulling at me all day long demanding attention. And then sometimes it was like an unabated linebacker who rushed offsides, didn't stop at the whistle, and blindsided me with relish. It's funny, but not so funny, how pain, even though it has been a part of us for years, can show up with such renewed intensity that it literally knocks the breath out of us. We feel its raw impact all over again.

So how did I deal with this pain?

I tried to pray it away. It stayed.

I tried to ignore it. It stayed.

For a short period of time, I tried to drink it away. It stayed.

I hoped that time would make it better. It didn't.

I hoped that the many good things in my life would cancel it out. They didn't.

I tried to distract myself from it. It would patiently wait through my distraction and then come back.

Often, a long amount of time would pass without me feeling the pain, so I was lulled into thinking that it was permanently gone. But it would inevitably show up again. I was becoming so tired of the surprise visits by the uninvited guest who I did not purposely open the door to, but who would find a way to get in.

Something different finally happened, though, when my familiar pain showed up. I greeted it with a resigned "hello," looked it in the eyes, and then did something I had never done before. I sat with it.

I did not try to make it leave. I did not resist it. I did not reach for a distraction. I did not begin to pray. I did not pour a drink. I did not try to meditate. I sat with it. And I'm almost sure I heard the pain say, "It's about time."

What happened when I sat with my pain? I felt it. Felt it hard. Felt it grip my heart. Felt it grip my stomach. Felt it overwhelm me. But I consciously made myself just sit and feel the pain without resisting it. And after I did that for awhile, I addressed it by simply saying, "You've been trying to get my attention for a very long time. Why? What is it you've been trying to tell me." And then I listened. I listened because it finally struck me that the pain was a messenger. It was a relentless messenger that was NEVER going away until I listened to what it had to say. As Rumi said, "These pains you feel are messengers. Listen to them."

Sitting with our pain is such a simple act and yet it can be one of the hardest things to do. So here are some tips to help you do it:

1. Sit with your pain.
2. Feel it.

There is nothing complicated about sitting with your pain. It's as easy/hard as just sitting with it. And each time, which might be a hundred times at first, you start to resist it, tell yourself, "No, this time I'm going to be different. I'm going to feel it."

(I'm going to interject this important note. If you have been abused or have suffered a severe type of pain, like the loss of a child or unexpected loss of a spouse or loved one, suffer from PTSD or any other type of severe pain that you have felt intensely for years, please don't try to sit with your pain by yourself. I believe it would be vital for you to have a professional counselor or very trusted, wise spiritual mentor aid you while sitting with your pain. Godspeed, because I can't imagine how hard it would be to sit with that kind of pain. But I believe it is necessary.)

I decided to sit with my pain after reading a chapter in the book *Love Warrior* by Glennon Doyle Melton. A friend who I frequently exchange books with gave it to me to read. I wasn't interested in reading it, though. So it sat beside my chair for months. But one day, for some reason, I decided to look at it. I randomly turned to a chapter in the middle of the book and started reading. It was the chapter in which Melton described how she sat with her pain. The chapter was a message to me. It was time for me to do what she had done. It was time for me to sit my pain and feel it.

Since doing this, close friends have described how they have recently sat with their pain, too. It's been amazing to hear their brave stories because they are dealing with much more severe pain than me. And it has been an affirmation to me that this is an important step for people to take in order to be healed and become balanced again.

Do you know what happened after I sat with my pain? It came back. But it did not overwhelm me. On a few occasions, it started to and I would feel a sense of dread. Then I would breathe and remember to let myself feel it, almost like I was just observing it, without trying to push it away. It was still finishing the message it was sent to tell me. So I still listened. Its visits are less and less frequent though.

When the author of *Love Warrior* sat with her pain, it was in the middle of a yoga class. The teacher recognized what was happening and did not interrupt the process. When class was over, the teacher simply said, "That - what you just did? That is the journey of the Warrior. Now, don't forget to breathe. You need to remember to breathe."

To sit with pain takes courage. It is the act of a warrior.

But it's not the pain you are actually at war with. It is yourself. And the irony of being a warrior, in this case, is the aspect of surrender. Because when you surrender to pain, you actually surrender to yourself. You call a truce and finally sit at the table with pain, and then you make yourself listen to what pain has to say. It is both an active and passive moment that sets off a revolution towards freedom.

Pain is not an enemy sent to destroy us. It is a messenger sent to keep us from destroying ourselves. This is such a vital distinction to make. Pain is trying to get us to hear what deep down we already know - that we have become imbalanced and have to change if we want to be healthy and at ease again. "Your pain is the breaking of the shell that encloses your understanding. It is the bitter potion by which the physician within you heals your sick self. Therefore, trust the physician and drink his remedy in silence and tranquility," Kahlil Gibran. I don't think sitting with your pain will always be done in silence or tranquility as Gibran describes. But I do believe pain is trying to bring us a remedy.

I realize that some of you will not want to sit with your pain. Not because you think it will be too hard. But because you have learned to identify so much with your pain that you have no desire or intention of letting it go. It has become too much a part of your story. It has become a large part of who you think you are. But I'm reminding you that you are not your pain. Pain is a messenger. It is not you. It does not want to be you. It only wants to speak to you and then be gone.

I was with a friend recently who was experiencing a bit of a meltdown. She was really upset, and as she cried she brought up a painful situation from her past. She angrily said, "I am so 'effed up by that!" I listened to her vent, offered encouragement, and helped her calm down. I knew it was not the right time to tell her what I was really thinking, but I knew I eventually needed to. A few days later, I got the opportunity to talk to her again. As we talked about her recent meltdown, I said, "You know how you said that you are still so screwed up by what happened to you? I don't believe you when you say that. You know why? Because that awful thing that happened to you, that you claim is still screwing you up - that's not meant to be a part of your current story anymore. Deep down, you want to and are going to let go of that event." And we talked about how she could do that.

I was not marginalizing the event that had caused her pain and was causing her to still feel messed up. But we sometimes have the strange desire to identify with our pain more than we desire to identify with our true selves. Sometimes it's easier, or at least it feels easier, to be a victim rather than to be whole. Being a victim of our circumstances allows us to temporarily escape our responsibilities. But if we aren't careful, the momentary victimhood turns into a part of our identity that we cling to. It becomes who we think we are, inhibiting us from being who we really are. We fool ourselves into thinking that nursing the pain, or the memory of the event that caused us pain, is easier than moving on from it. Weird, I know. But sometimes we're weird like that.

Being a victim is also a way we seek attention. We seek attention and perpetual help from others rather than taking steps to let go of our pain so we can become well again. In essence, we'd rather keep metaphorically lying in a fetal position than standing up, pulling up our bootstraps, and getting on with our lives. So let me help you remember that you are not your pain. You are so much more than your pain. And you are not the events that have happened to you. You are not even the responses to the events that have happened to you. You are so much more than that. Yes, the events hurt you, shaped you, sharpened you, changed you, improved you, exhausted you, impeded you, propelled you, maybe even almost killed you. Even so, you are so much more than your painful past.

Perhaps this chapter will be for you what the chapter in *Love Warrior* was for me; a perfectly timed catalyst. A defining moment that spurs you to sit with your pain, feel it, and listen to it. Perhaps listen to it again, and again, and again. And then finally watch it leave.

When pain leaves there will be a void, a vacuum. And vacuums must be filled. That's a law of the universe. So intentionally fill the vacuum with positive feelings and choices. Some of the things I filled my vacuum with were feelings and actions of strength, empowerment, and determination. And light. I always have room for more light in life.

I pray that God would infuse you with strength and courage to sit with your pain. May you finally feel your pain without reaching for anything or anyone to distract you from it. And after you feel it, I pray you would hear its message and that you would have the courage and wisdom to implement whatever steps you need to take to become balanced and at ease again. I pray that your pain would finally be a gateway to your healing. And when your healing comes, I pray that the lightness of your being will, in turn, bring healing to others.

Remember to Stop Judging

I used to carry the biggest chip on my shoulder. It was big. Huge. And it was labeled, "I'm Right and If You Don't Agree With Me Then You Are Wrong." I'm a little embarrassed, okay a lot embarrassed, that I carried such a chip.

The chip stemmed from the way I view life, especially the spiritual aspects of life. I am a truth-seeker. At one point in my life, though, truth was the bottom line and if feelings got hurt over what I thought was the truth, or theologies shot down, or traditions were broken, I didn't care. Truth was truth and people just needed to deal with it. Like I said, I'm a little embarrassed by that chip-carrying era of my life.

I'm still a truth-seeker. But I seek it for myself. And if the truth I find helps other people, so be it. But if it doesn't, then so be it, too. I can be right without anyone else agreeing with me. The way I reached this point was when a dear friend of mine knocked the chip off of my shoulder with one potent sentence. She said, "Camie, you can be right without everyone else being wrong."

Wow. I don't think I've ever been nailed that accurately, that hard, yet that gently. I'm so thankful that my friend loved me enough to tell me exactly what I needed to hear. She saved me from my foolish pride. She saved me from judging people's beliefs, viewpoints, and actions.

We often judge people because of their failure to believe or act in a given situation the way we would. Some of us habitually measure people according to our view points, strengths, abilities, beliefs, and tendencies rather than accepting them for who they are.

Each of us has strengths and weaknesses. What I struggle with might be the easiest thing in the world for someone else to overcome and vice versa. It's unfair to judge each other, not only because we seldom know the entire story of what someone is going through, but also because no one has the same set of strengths and weaknesses as we do. The only true Judge obviously is God, because He is the only One who sees all and knows all, down to the details of what our strengths and weaknesses are. He might be giving us applause and fist bumps in certain situations, while people are judging us, because He realizes what a feat it was, given our weaknesses, to do or at least attempt to do what we did. That's not to say that He doesn't expect us to improve in our weak areas, nor does He brush aside every mistake we make, but He is slow to judge because He knows us better than we know ourselves.

I recently heard the phrase "you do you" and liked it. It's

a good reminder to be yourself. It's also a reminder to let everyone else be themselves, too, hopefully without judging them.

My kids don't get overly frustrated with people, but when they do, and when they vent about it, the point I try to help them see goes a little something like this: "You know what? That person just has a different personality type than you. And although, you want people to see things from your point of view and react to situations like you would, sometimes they won't because of their different personality types. Some personality types you're really going to like and connect with, and some not so much. But the point is, we shouldn't spend a lot of time or energy getting upset with people for simply being who they are."

I can give that kind of advice because a few years ago I made the decision to try to stop expecting people to live up to my expectations. I started accepting people for who they were rather than expecting them to be who I thought they should be. I suppose I had started living according to the maxim "you do you" before it had become a popular catch-phrase.

If we are honest with ourselves, then we'd probably admit that we spend too much time assigning our personality traits to other people. We want and expect people to act like us. When they don't, we get disappointed with them, or worse, we think that something is wrong with them. But in reality all they are doing is being themselves.

I have the sweetest Golden Retriever named Bella. When I come home or wake up, she runs to look for something to put in her mouth to bring to me. Often what she brings me is something that she's not supposed to have. But I've stopped scolding her when she brings me something she isn't supposed to have because it occurred to me that she was just being herself. She was retrieving. That is who she is. It is her instinct. So I firmly but gently tell her to drop whatever it is that she's not supposed to have. But then I love on her and tell her, "You're such a good retriever."

Bella's actions and my reaction to her are a reminder to ask myself if I'm accepting people for who they are rather than expecting them to be who I think they should be. I could get annoyed at Bella for retrieving, but I get a kick out of it instead. Granted, often dogs are easier to be around than people, but Bella constantly reminds me that I should try to give my fellow human beings as much acceptance as I give her.

We can never completely relate to another person's journey in life. But that lack of relating shouldn't lead to judgment. Also, it might help to remember that people are mirrors, often reflecting our own shortcomings back to us. The things we often get the most upset by in other people, are what we need to remedy in ourselves.

There are not many things in life that I can guarantee will happen, but people being mirrors in our lives is guaranteed to happen. People we encounter are sent to help us see ourselves as we truly are. But sometimes we choose to quickly look away rather than see the true reflection of ourselves. If we are brave enough, though, we will look in the mirror that people show us. If we are even braver, we will honestly assess our reflection. And if we are even braver still, we will work on changing our faults that are reflected.

The Baal Shem Tov taught that no encounter is by chance. He said that every person we encounter has been placed in our lives as a mirror. He said, "If a person witnesses the degradation of his fellow, he must realize that he, too, suffers from the same lack in one form or another. Otherwise, why would Divine Providence have caused him to see his fellow's failings? Obviously, to open his eyes to something he must correct in himself . . . Even if it is in the subtlest of forms within himself."

Since we are human, we are going to make mistakes and have faults. That is part of the human condition. Even so, our humanity is an asset. It is not shameful. We will fall. But the greatness is in getting up. We can utilize the fall. Elevate the fall. God expects us to fall. But He also hopes that we will and expects us to get up. So if He hopes that, then we should do the same rather than judging each other.

Each of us is on a journey to get back to our true selves, which I like to refer to as our "Genesis selves." Have you ever asked God to help you become that person? Your Genesis self? I have. I wonder what His intention was for me the first time He thought of me. Whether we realize it or not, our life is a journey to get back to the person He first thought of when He created us. Our journey is to make *teshuva*, which means to return. How many steps is it going to take to return to our original selves? One? A thousand? A million? And how many of those steps are going to be forward? And how many will be backward?

We never know when encountering or observing another person, which step he is on? Maybe he is taking a giant step forward. Or instead, maybe he is tumbling end-over-end backward. If he is, who are we to judge without knowing what caused him to tumble?

My journey, my life, my problems, my failures, my accomplishments, and my advancements are no more nor less important than yours. They are just different. We entered this world with a particular mission to accomplish, which includes getting back to ourselves. But our mission also includes making this world a better place. Remember the piece of paper that Rabbi Simcha Bunim always carried that said, "For my sake, the world was created"? Accompanying that belief is the idea of responsibility. In essence, if the world was created for our sake, then we are supposed to act as if we are the lone gardener or caretaker of the world. We are supposed to have a sense that we are the only ones who can fix the world. And the first and most powerful place to start fixing the world is by fixing ourselves. Fix a portion of ourselves, and we fix a portion of the world. Reveal more of our light, and we diminish darkness in the world. This sense of responsibility is not so we will feel overwhelmed by such a large task or feel prideful that we are the only ones who can fix the world. It's to remind us of how vital our role is because no one else can do exactly what we were sent here to do.

As I said, everyone's journey back to themselves is different. So, therefore, each of us will experience restoration, awakening, and healing in different ways. And everyone's mission to repair the world is different. So it's not important how the journey and mission looks, but that the journey and mission are embarked upon. Focusing on our journey and mission leaves little time to judge and criticize others. And frankly, if we do judge and criticize others, it just makes our journey and mission that much harder.

I pray that we will remember that life is reciprocal and the way that we judge others is the way that we will be judged. Help us, God, to be merciful and slow to judge. Help us remember that You are the One True Judge. And if for some reason we are ever called upon to judge a situation, help us do it with an attitude of wanting what is best for our fellow human being. Help us return to our true selves. And help us have a solid sense of what our mission is and have the resources, confidence, tenacity, support, brazenness, and perhaps a little touch of craziness, if we need it, to accomplish it.

Remember to Be Kind

I have a pet peeve about myself and other people. It bothers me if people, myself included, profess to be religious or spiritual but aren't kind. What is the point of being religious or spiritual if it doesn't make us kinder? Kindness is not trivial. It's the bedrock of the world.

Abraham is the patriarch of monotheism. Four thousand years ago, he was the first person to believe that there was One driving force and power behind every action in the universe. As a child, he began to ask questions about his observances of the world. He eventually concluded that there was only One Supreme Being in control of everything. It was a dramatic conclusion considering he lived in a world filled with idolatry and cult worship and that his father sold idols.

Abraham was called "Abraham the Hebrew." The root word for "Hebrew" is "ivri" which literally means "to cross over." The sages teach that this represents Abraham's willingness and boldness to cross over from the normative, social acceptance of idolatry to the belief in One God. As a truth-seeker, Abraham was willing to cross over and stand alone in his beliefs.

Yet, Abraham was known for something even more profound than setting the precedent of believing that God was the One Source for everything. He was known for his attribute of *chesed*, of kindness. It was the characteristic that he valued most and wanted to pass on to his family. Maybe like me, you consider yourself a "child of Abraham" because you believe in One God. But do we act like Abraham? Are we kind?

A story in Genesis describes how Abraham was weak and in pain after being circumcised at the age of 99, but despite his discomfort, he longed for travelers to come by his tent so that he could offer kindness to them. My favorite part of the story is how Abraham treated God when he saw the travelers coming toward his tent. He put God "on hold." Abraham was interacting with God, but when he saw that he actually had an opportunity to apply his spirituality and make it relevant in the physical dimension, he literally jumped at the chance. He quickly told God to "hold on!" so that he could interact with man instead of interacting with Him. I love that. And I think that God did too.

I'm more prone to be a thinker than a doer. Abraham's eagerness to be kind, his desire to run to do good, reminds me to ask myself, "What's the point of all my spiritual contemplations and revelations if I don't actually apply what I learn? And one of the most profound ways to translate my thoughts into actions is through acts of kindness.

I'm a reserved person around most people. But I make myself be kind even to people who I don't know. Maybe it doesn't seem like much, but I smile at nearly every person I encounter throughout the day whether I know them or not. Smiling is such a simple thing to do, but I think that it's a powerful act. It's a way to acknowledge the light of God in others.

Sometimes I don't only smile at strangers, but I wave at them enthusiastically, too. If I'm in my backyard when the garbage truck comes down the alley to dump the garbage container and I see the driver, I smile and wave at him hoping he somehow perceives how thankful I am for him. Honestly, if I could, I would run and hug his neck, but that would probably be overkill. I just wish I could make him feel like the most important person in the world and let him know how much I appreciate him. How gross it would quickly become if no one came to collect the garbage and it just kept piling up. The garbage collector makes my life so much better. I can't imagine trying to write a book, have a moment with God, or really do anything in my house, if it was full of garbage.

A small act of kindness that I've recently started implementing is paying for a soldier's meal if I see him or her in a restaurant. If the soldier has already paid for his meal, I get him a gift card to use the next time he's there. As I mentioned, I'm a fairly reserved person, so it's not "natural" for me to approach strangers and talk to them. But I greatly admire military personal, so I make myself get out of my comfort zone because even though it's a small way to thank them, I want to show them that I appreciate their service to our country.

My acts of kindness aren't remarkable or noteworthy. They are just representative of what so many other people do. I encounter kind people all of the time. Often I catch myself thinking, "People are just so nice!" They really are. And they constantly inspire me to be kind.

I'm inspired by teachers in my small community who help take care of students from low-income families. Upon discovering that students are living in a home with no heat during the winter months, or have only one pair of socks, or do not have a coat that fits, teachers have immediately reached into their own pockets and paid the electrical bill or bought warm clothing for the children.

Also in my small community are several couples who have become foster parents. I am in awe of them. These couples have children of their own, work outside of the home, and have very busy schedules. But because of kindness, they have opened their homes and their hearts to take care of and raise children who need loving homes. This type of kindness amazes me. I can smile or wave at people all day long. But people near me and throughout the world, are kind in ways that have such a huge, direct impact on people. I strive to be that type of kind person, too.

We all have different personality types, so the ways in which we are kind will vary. When I was visiting friends in Israel, one of them commented on the kindness of people he encounters in America. He said, "Many of you seem nice in a sweet, "sticky" kind of way. You are always smiling or asking, 'How are you?' Here in Israel, we don't always act as nice. But we would do anything and everything in our power for you if you ever needed help." His words resonated with me. Smiles are nice, but actions are nicer. He was an elite IDF soldier, who now teaches self-defense classes to people around the world. He is one of the toughest, yet funniest, nicest people I have ever met. As my daughter and I commented to each other later, he has the kindest eyes. Yet, his truest kindness is through actions. He would do anything to help another person.

The world benefits from all of our various ways of being kind. From powerful, wealthy, intellectual people to the lowly, poor, not-so-educated people, most of us feel the same thing when someone is kind to us. We feel good. We feel like the world is a little better place. We are reminded that we really are "all in this together." We remember what we are, but often forget - we remember that we are all connected.

I think kindness is a superpower that we forget that we have. We can get so caught up in our worries, concerns, needs, and responsibilities that we forget to be kind. Or we allow ourselves to get into a habit of being mean or indifferent rather than being kind. Or we are just too prideful to be kind. But kindness is powerful in the sense that it makes us other-centered instead of being self-centered. It prevents us from becoming callous, even when it seems like callousness is a necessary form of protection if we perceive the world as a hard, unsafe place.

Micah 6:8 is a concise reminder of what God expects from us: to do justice, love kindness, and walk humbly with Him. Do we meet those expectations? Do we love being kind?

Abraham always looked for "sparks" in people. He saw the good in people and reminded them of their potential. That is the ultimate act of kindness; to remind someone of his or her true self. Abraham held up a mirror to people and in essence said, "Look, this is the real you. Be that. Don't be the counterfeit you." Abraham facilitated people's reconnection to their true selves by making them aware of their original holy sparks within. He was remarkably good at reminding people how extraordinary they were, full of wonderful traits such as goodness and kindness. By reminding people of what was really inside of them, he reminded them that acting in negative ways was not consistent with who they truly were.

Rahab and the two spies, Caleb and Pinchas, saw the sparks in each other as conveyed in the story from the Book of Joshua about the spies going into the Land of Israel to observe Jericho. Rahab, Caleb, and Pinchas reminded each other of their potential. They helped each other return to their true selves. Caleb and Pinchas helped Rahab remember that she was not destined to remain a prostitute. Instead, she was destined to marry Joshua and be the progenitor of prophets, which included Isaiah and Zechariah. And Rahab had the boldness and the clarity to remind the spies that their destiny was to take possession of the Land of Israel. They all imitated Abraham by seeing the true essence in each other - by seeing the sparks in each other and fanning them to a flame.

Adam had the ability to see the true essence of all the animals that God created. He was given the task of naming each kind. As he saw their essence, he named each accordingly. On that note, when we see the true essence of individuals, the names/labels we have for them will change. Have you ever been encouraged by someone who saw you for who you really were? Few things are more powerful than someone labeling us as strong, smart, powerful, full of potential, capable and a whole slew of other amazing labels that describe our true essence.

Aaron was also known for seeing people's potential. He accepted people where they were at, yet simultaneously expected them to become the best versions of themselves. The almond branch staff that he carried represented what he expected of people. He expected them to blossom. He never looked down upon anyone. Instead, he looked at them eye-to-eye. What an amazing gift to give a fellow human being - to look them eye-to-eye. Aaron's act of kindness to everyone he encountered was believing in them so much that they finally started believing in themselves. I've been blessed to have "Aarons" in my life; people who have helped me blossom. People who fanned my sparks of potential to flame. People who accepted me for who I was, yet knew I could be even better. I pray that same blessing for you, that you would have people in your life who help you reach your potential. I also pray that, in turn, you would become a student of Aaron and begin seeing people as he did and help them reach their potential.

Psalm 89:3 says, "The world is built with *chesed* (kindness)." Kindness is choosing to build another person up instead of tearing them down. We do this each time we encourage someone to become better versions of themselves rather than judging and criticizing them for being less than who we think they should be. Every time we build someone up with kindness, we emulate God Who is always seeing and expecting the best in us and from us.

God being God has no needs. He didn't create us and the world because He needed us. He wanted us. He had no one outside of Himself to give to. So God's primary purpose for creating us and the world was to bestow kindness upon us. Therefore, the most profound way we emulate God is by bestowing kindness upon each other.

The sage Hillel once asked, "If I am only for myself, what am I?" Maybe you've fooled yourself into thinking otherwise, but your natural inclination, since you are made in the image of God, is to be kind. We just forget that sometimes. Kindness reminds us that we are here for other reasons than for ourselves. We are here for each other. And like Abraham, we should go out of our way to look for ways to be kind to each other.

I had the honor of hearing my friend speak about his beloved mother at her funeral recently. Her name was Grace. And from what he said, and others who spoke about her said, it was easy to see that Grace emulated God. She lived up to the Merriam-Webster definition of her name. She gave "unmerited divine assistance to humans for their regeneration." She was the living word of grace. She was a child of Abraham. She was a student of Aaron. She was the hand of God who built people. She constantly created an environment of love, support, and encouragement to help people reach their potential. As my friend ended his eulogy, he read the lyrics from the U2 song "Grace" which he thought so aptly captured the true essence of all that she was. The song says:

Grace
She takes the blame
She covers the shame
Removes the stain
It could be her name

It's the name for a girl
It's also a thought that
Changed the world

What left a mark
No longer stains
Because grace makes beauty
Out of ugly things

Grace finds beauty in everything
Grace finds goodness
In everything

Dear God, help us be like Grace in every sense of the word. Help us be like Abraham and run to be kind, like Rahab, Caleb, and Pinchas who fanned the sparks in each other, and like Aaron who saw and expected the best in others. Most of all, help us be extensions of You, bestowing kindness on all who we encounter. Help us be kind in a world where people are starving for an act of kindness. Rather than being like wrecking balls destroying others with our words, thoughts, or actions, help us be carpenters who build up the world with kindness. Remind us to use our superpower of kindness any and every chance that we get.

Remember to Be Happy

This might seem like a strange way to start a chapter about being happy, but I have to begin the chapter by saying that we will never be completely happy and there is a place of longing in us that will never be completely filled, until we experience complete unification with God. And even though we can become more and more unified with God each and every day, until redemption happens, which will be a time when we all come out of our restrictive state and no longer experience the illusion of separation from Him, we won't be completely happy. As Rabbi Noah Weinberg said, "No human being is totally satisfied unless he's in touch with the transcendent dimension. When all is said and done, what we each seek is to reach out of this finite world and connect with the infinite. To become one with God."

There is an insatiable ache in us that simply can't be filled by anything else but God. I really believe that. Therefore, I believe that seeking happiness and fulfillment is in vain unless we have a relationship with God. Connection with Source is vital and foundational for our happiness.

But on the other hand, God created a big, incredible, fantastic world for us to enjoy, too. I think He wants us to and expects us to live life with enthusiasm and to experience life in a state of happiness. So, as the Partridge Family used to tell me every day after school, "Come on, get happy."

Are you happy? Do you want to be happy? Do you think you deserve to be happy? Do you think people who seek happiness are shallow or misguided? Do you think God wants us to be happy? These are the types of questions a facilitator asked at a book club I was invited to sit in on one evening. We paused a little bit to ponder her questions and then she asked us, "What would make you happy?" An answer came to me immediately. As people in the group shared what would make them happy, though, I thought, "Uh oh, maybe I need to change my answer." They were sharing very spiritual things. But I decided to be honest, so when it was my turn to share I said, "What would make me happy is to be able to go to as many MLB baseball games as I want to go to." A part of me felt like I should put on a giant scarlet "S" for shallowness for giving that kind of answer. Yet, another part of me realized that I had come a long way to arrive at that kind of answer.

I am a very spiritual person. So much so, that sometimes I lose sight of living with fullness in the physical world. Realizing and admitting that going to baseball games would make me happy, was actually a spiritual advancement for me. I've often thought that I would have made a good monk or nun. I kind of like being cloistered. But something different started happening to me. I began to feel beckoned to engage more in the physical world to balance my spirituality. So what if I was devoutly spiritual, yet was missing out on living the other parts of my life with passion? The more I pondered my imbalance, the more I realized that I wanted to live the rest of my life alive, experiencing more of life. I wanted to be happy, not just because I was connected to God, but because I was enjoying all that He created, too (and yes, I believe He created baseball).

My answer to the question, "What would make you happy?" is a reminder that none of our journeys in life will look the same. Someone who didn't know me could have easily thought my answer indicated that I was a shallow person. It didn't indicate that, though. It was actually a healthy step for me to admit that I have desires and that those desires don't make me shallow, but are simply indicative that I'm human. The realization that my desires were just another avenue for connection with God was a spiritual advancement for me.

Psalm 100 reminds us to serve God with gladness. We have so many reasons to be glad. Glad that we are breathing. Glad that we have food to eat. Glad that we are loved. Glad that we experience beauty. Glad that we experience hardships that birth better versions of ourselves.

Glad that we have an awareness of God. Basically, just glad that we exist. When we let the primal point of our happiness be the fact that we exist in God - that we live, move, and have our being in Him - then all the extras in our lives, like getting to go to baseball games, are icing on the cake. And I'm okay with finally admitting that I really like and want more of the icing.

Icing and all, I have so many reasons to be happy. But sometimes I let my problems and concerns overshadow my happiness. Which I think is completely normal. But only for awhile. I don't want to perpetually let my happiness be overshadowed by the concerns in my life.

Jewish sages teach that happiness breaks through all boundaries and constrictions. They also teach that prayers accompanied by happiness and praise are more powerful than approaching God in tears. I think part of the reason that is true is because sometimes being happy takes a great amount of faith in the midst of our needs and problems. It also is, in a sense, a foretelling, a prediction that even though circumstances don't look the way we think they should, everything is going to work out the way it should. Being happy sometimes requires cultivation. It requires deliberateness. Sometimes we have to say to ourselves, "Even though I don't feel happy, I'm going to feel happy."

Judaism has one entire month devoted to the cultivation

of happiness. The month is called Adar. The tagline for Adar is, "When Adar begins, our joy increases." What I want that to mean is that right at the stroke of midnight on the 1st of Adar, "bam!" everything becomes hunky-dory in our lives and we automatically feel happy. I wish. That's not what it means, though. It means that Adar is a time, despite our circumstances or along with our circumstances, to remind ourselves to "come on, get happy."

One of my favorite ways to cultivate happiness is by watching funny sitcoms like *Seinfeld* or *The Office*. Or by watching funny videos with my daughter that people post on Twitter. People are so funny. And it's amazing how a few minutes of laughter can "reset" us and enable us to see our concerns or problems from a better, more positive perspective. I also have friends in my life who are naturally funny. I love being around them. I usually leave with my stomach hurting because we laugh so hard when we are together. What makes you laugh? Whatever it is, do more of that. Proverbs says that a happy heart is like taking a good dose of medicine. I think we'd all benefit from increasing our dosage of laughter.

Not to get too hippyish, but humans have vibrational frequencies. Everything, in fact, has a vibrational frequency. That's because even though matter appears to be solid, it is not. We, along with everything else, are made of moving particles which emit frequency. Everything is energy. Guess what causes our vibrational frequency/our energy to be at a higher, healthier level? Easy answer. Being and feeling happy.

Happiness energizes us. It motivates us. It makes us feel more confident. Better than a protein shake - happiness is pure energy. We are better at operating in our day-to-day lives when we feel motivated, confident, and are full of positive energy. We are even better at doing the things we don't like doing when we feel happy.

When the month of Adar begins, our stresses, frustrations, pains, and problems don't all just disappear. Adar reminds us that despite what's going on in our lives or in the world, we still need to be happy. Not because we are pretending that we don't have problems. But we learn and acknowledge that choosing to be happy helps us through our problems.

Judaism teaches the principle of *chitzonit mi'orrer pi'nimiut*, which means the external awakens the internal. It means that it is possible to develop an emotional state by acting as if we are already in that state. Maybe you've heard it said as, "Fake it 'til you make it." Yes, getting to do fun, good things, that fulfill our hearts' desires is a huge source of happiness. But underlying happiness is a state of mind rather than a by-product of getting something we want.

God/the Universe is a mirror. When we feel and express happiness just because we've decided to be happy that we're alive, it's as if God says, "Look at her. She's so happy about just being alive that I'm going to give her even more reasons to be happy." Happiness attracts happiness. Really. I dare you to get happy.

God, I pray that You will remind us to be happy. When we awaken in the morning, help us greet ourselves, the day, and You with a feeling of happiness. I pray that You would give us our hearts' desires and that we would accept moments and events in life that induce happiness. But more than that, I pray that You would help us be happy to be alive. And still, even more than that, I pray that we would be so happy to be connected to You.

Remember to Hang On

Sometimes what I've written about in this book goes out the window momentarily, and it seems that all I can do is hang on to my sanity. I feel anything but lighthearted, happy, and peaceful. Thankfully, these kinds of moments are passing and aren't the "norm" in my life.

One time, though, I literally had to hang on to my sanity. I'm a competitive person. So when my older sister delivered her babies without an epidural, guess what the competitor in me thought? I thought that I could do the same. After all, I was only in labor for an hour-and-a-half when I delivered my first baby. So the second time around I thought, "No problem! How hard can it really be to have a baby naturally?"

During the first thirty minutes of interval not-so-hard contractions, I remember thinking what a good decision I had made not to get an epidural. "I've got this!" I happily and a little smugly thought. Then the labor pains intensified. It was a pain that I did not know a human could experience, much less endure. And it just kept getting worse. "What have I done?!?" I thought to myself. Or maybe I yelled it. It's hard to remember those kinds of details. "And why haven't I had this baby yet!?! It's been over an hour-and-a-half!"

As the contractions got stronger I asked, or rather demanded, in a begging kind of way for the nurse to give me an epidural. "Honey, it's way too late for that," she said. It was, without a doubt, the meanest thing anyone has ever said to me.

When the contractions got to the point of ripping out my lower back, I lifted off the bed in pain. I think it was what's known as "writhing." Yep, I writhed. All pride and any sense of decorum were the furthest things from my mind. Because at that point I remember thinking that I was about to go insane. Literally, insane. And I was pretty okay with that. Anything to stop the pain, because I was fairly certain that my body and mind could not stand one more second of it.

Then the moment came that made all the pain worth it. Of course, you know, without me having to tell you, what that moment was. It might sound like a cliché, but to each woman who tells the story of childbirth it is so much more than a cliché. The moment my baby was born, everything was forgotten, except that I was finally holding him. All the pain was replaced by more relief and thankfulness than I'd ever felt.

There are many events in my life that I don't remember

well, if at all. But I remember the birth of my son vividly. I remember feeling him being born; that moment when he finally, and ironically, slipped out so easily after such a painful labor. It was the best feeling in the world. One that I will never forget. That one moment made every second of pain worth it.

We are at a juncture that ancient writers and prophets referred to as "birth pains." A time of transition. A time right before something spectacular will be born: redemption. After such an intense labor, peace will finally and ironically "slip" easily into the world. That's why sometimes life hurts so much that collectively and individually we think we are on the brink of insanity. We wonder if we or the world can endure one more second of pain.

I heard an analogy about this particular time in history that has stayed with me about a spring that was being pulled preternaturally. It was being pulled so hard and so far down that it was surprising that the spring did not break. And just when you thought the spring could not be pulled down any further, it was. It kept being pulled, and pulled, and pulled. It was well past what should have been its breaking point.

We are at that point. The world is a spring being pulled so hard and so far down, that it seems like it has passed its breaking point. And that, my dear fellow human beings, is why life seems so heavy sometimes. It's because in some ways it is. In some ways, it's heavier than it ever has been before. And in the heavy moments, we plagiarize the singing prophet Cohen and take our broken Hallelujahs to God as pleading praise proffered in hopes of reminding Him how dire our situation is, or at least seems.

But something is about to happen. So please keep holding on. The spring is about to be released. And when it's released its upward projectile will never stop. It. Will. Never. Stop. Rising. The descent is for the sake of ascent. We will be released forever from our current constrictive state. We will finally get back to our true state of being. We will get back to our Genesis selves. We will get back to perfect union with God. We will get back to paradise. Our finite minds can't really comprehend all that this means. But if it is anything like the birth of a child, we will instantly understand that all of our pain was worth it.

We often walk a tightrope in this world. It's a balancing act of staying steady in the midst of love, happiness, and peace mixed with the uncertainty, hopelessness, and fear we feel during moments when the spring is pulled harder and further down. Life is often a combination of exhilaration and exhaustion, much like the combination I felt after delivering my son.

My sister took a picture of me minutes after my son was born. I have a grin on my face that is my signature look of satisfaction. When my dad saw the picture later, he said, "You look pretty proud of yourself in that picture. Like you just accomplished the best thing in the world. Which I suppose you did just that."

I have a feeling that we will have a similar expression on our faces when life is all said and done. We will be proud of ourselves. We will have a look and a feeling of satisfaction from accomplishing the best thing in the world - the feat of having lived as incredible beings of lightness in a world that often felt dark and heavy. But we will have done it and done it well.

So keep holding on during moments when you feel heaviness instead of lightheartedness. You are on earth, at this very moment, for a reason. And if all of those who have gone before us could tell us something, I think they would say:

Don't give up. Don't stay down. Get up. Always get up. There is too much to do. You are almost finished. But you've got to do your part 'til the very end.

When you feel heaviness, think of it as all of our hands on your shoulders, not to push you down, but to help you square your shoulders as we look you in the eyes and say, "You've got this! Don't you dare quit."

You feel us. You feel the expectations, hopes, and desires of all who have gone before you. And deep down you know that the work we did before you won't be complete unless you do your part, too. Your love. Your trust. Your work. Your persistence. Your faith. Your connection to God. Your healing. Your kindness. Your happiness. It is all so vital. It is all so necessary.

Lastly, don't forget to smile. And laugh. Ever once and a while, tilt your head back at the sky and laugh at the wonderment and strangeness of this journey you are on. Predict the future with your laughter. Predict that it's all going to be okay, in fact, better than okay. It's going to be better than you could ever think or imagine.

Along with those who have gone before us, of course, God is watching us, too. But perhaps what we don't realize, is that He is watching us with the intent of waiting for that one final act of faith, or love, or kindness, or who really knows what it will be, from one of us and when He sees it, He will think, "That's it! That's the moment we've all been waiting for." Then He will let go of the spring. And redemption will begin. It will begin, and just like Him, it will be unending. It. Will. Never. End.

Until that time, please God, help us keep holding on. Help us have faith that since it is Your hand pulling the spring down, that it will, of course, be Your hand that will finally release us from this state of constriction that has kept us from being fully unified with You. Help us trust Your timing. If there is anything that we can do to hasten the release of the spring, show us. And give us the courage, the resources, and the tenacity to do it. We long for You. We miss You. And until we can be fully reunited with You, on every level of our being, please give us a heart full of light.

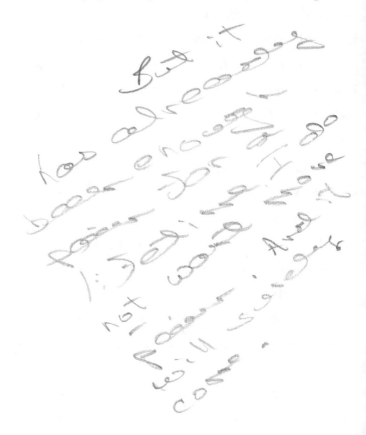